100 GREATEST

DISASTERS

D1514966

Michael Pollard

Grolier Educational

SHERMAN TURNPIKE, DANBURY, CONNECTICUT 06816

Published 1997
Grolier Educational
Danbury, CT 06816

Published for the school and library market
exclusively by Grolier Educational

© Dragon's World Ltd, 1995

Set ISBN 0–7172–7691–0
Volume ISBN 0–7172–7684–8

**Library of Congress
Cataloguing in Publication Data**
100 Greatest Disasters.
     p. cm.
     Includes index.
     Summary: Presents brief descriptions of the
world's greatest disasters, including the Yucatán
asteroid strike, Mount St. Helens, Chernobyl
nuclear accident, and the Challenger space
shuttle explosion.
     ISBN 0-7172-7684-8
     1. Disasters--Juvenile literature.
     [1. Disasters.]
D24.A22 1997
904'.7--dc21
                                        96-38056
                                        CIP
                                        AC

Editor: Kyla Barber
Designer: Mel Raymond
Picture Research: Josine Meijer
Art Director: John Strange
Editorial Director: Pippa Rubinstein

Printed in Italy

Contents

Introduction

The Earth on which we live seems, most of the time, a very solid, safe place where things happen as we expect them to happen. But once in a while an event takes place that reminds us that in some ways our Earth, one of billions of bodies that make up the universe, is very fragile. Its crust can move and split open, causing earthquakes and volcanoes. Its weather can suddenly deal deadly blows by way of hurricanes and floods. It is vulnerable to collisions with other bodies from space such as meteorites and comets.

About half of the one hundred greatest disasters described in this book had their origins in natural forces connected with the Earth's geology and climate. Some could have been predicted by studying earlier eruptions of volcanoes or the regular pattern of the world's weather. The Huang He or Yellow River in China, for example, has flooded regularly throughout history, bringing huge loss of life each time.

Other disasters were completely unexpected. One of the strongest earthquakes ever recorded, in New Madrid, Missouri, in 1811, took place in an area that had no previous history of tremors. No one could have foreseen the huge body from space that crashed near Tunguska in Siberia—fortunately without loss of life—in 1908. Such unexpected disasters show that, despite all our knowledge of the world we live in, it can still give us some grim surprises.

Natural disasters can spring from other causes. Some of the greatest killers in history have been diseases that swept uncontrollably across the world. In the days when the causes and spread of disease were not understood, these epidemics often lasted for years, bringing economic and social upheaval as they killed off productive workers and left the very old and the very young alone, weak and starving. Over most of the world, such epidemics as bubonic plague and cholera are now eliminated or controlled, but the appearance of AIDS was a reminder that we must continue to research and develop new cures for new illnesses.

A third group of disasters whose stories are told in this book resulted from human activity. Excluding wars— whose death toll, taken over history, exceeds those of every natural calamity —human greed or foolishness has brought catastrophe in countless ways.

Our thoughtless treatment of the environment, for example, has already laid waste large tracts of land, threatened to poison our atmosphere and water supplies, polluted the oceans, and driven to extinction rare plant and animal life. Most of this damage occurs slowly over many years, but occasionally an accident like the Bhopal chemical plant leakage in India in 1984 or the *Exxon Valdez* oil spill in 1989, bring immediate and

dramatic attention to the need to take more care of the world, for all our sakes.

Michael Pollard

OPPOSITE
TOP LEFT: The Irish famine of the 1840s.
TOP RIGHT: Kanto earthquake, Japan, 1923.
BOTTOM LEFT: Thinning of the ozone layer.

ABOVE: Hillsborough soccer tragedy, England, 1989.
BELOW: The sinking of the *Titanic*, 1912.

Permian extinctions
250 million years ago

Up to about 200 million years ago, there were no separate continents divided by oceans: there was one huge land mass that geologists call Pangea. This vast area was bursting with plant and animal life. At this time, before the appearance of the dinosaurs, the dominant land creatures were reptiles. Conifers and ferns were the most common plants. Geologists call this the Permian period.

Towards the end of the Permian period, a disaster of some kind overtook the world. No one can be sure what happened, but three-quarters of all plants and animals were destroyed. About one-third of the species living on Earth at that time disappeared. One theory is that there was a huge geological upheaval that either raised the land or lowered the sea level. Another guess is that at about this time Pangea began to split up into the continents we know today. This division of the great land mass could have brought about dramatic climatic changes that many species could not survive.

The extinction of such a large proportion of living things in the Permian period probably paved the way for the evolution of the dinosaurs, the first of which appeared between 200 and 135 million years ago. They were able to take advantage of the new conditions on Earth, and prospered for over 100 million years.

▼ The collision of an asteroid with the Earth could have caused the sort of disaster that resulted in the extinctions at the end of the Permian period.

The Yucatán asteroid strike

65 million years ago

About 65 million years ago a great natural event destroyed much of life on Earth. It ended the age of the dinosaurs, and wiped out most other species of plant and animal life on Earth.

In 1980, Professor Luis Alvarez of the University of California came up with a new theory about what might have happened. He suggested that the Earth was struck by a huge asteroid between 4 and 7 miles across, which landed on the Yucatán Peninsula in Mexico. The immense force with which the asteroid crashed to Earth created a vast crater and a dust cloud that blotted out the light of the Sun for many years.

Plants would have died, followed by the animals—including dinosaurs—that fed on them. Life gradually died out all over the darkened Earth. The layers of clay between rocks that were formed about 65 million years ago contain high levels of iridium, an element found in asteroids. So the atmosphere may have contained asteroid dust at that time.

▲ One of the giant dinosaurs looks on as an enormous asteroid plunges through the atmosphere and lands on the Earth's surface.

◀ Large plant-eating dinosaurs like *Apatosaurus* (center) would have been the first to suffer when the vegetation died. Meat-eaters like *Tyrannosaurus Rex* (foreground) would soon also die as their food supply disappeared.

Many other ideas have been put forward to explain the extinction of the dinosaurs. These range from a sudden change in the world's climate to the explosion of a star, which caused the Earth to be bathed in deadly radiation.

Barringer Crater

c. 50,000 BC

Near the town of Winslow in the heart of the Arizona desert there is a huge bowl-shaped crater 4,200 feet across and 575 feet deep. It is called the Barringer, or Meteor, Crater.

The Barringer Crater was formed about 50,000 years ago when a huge meteorite —a fragment of rock from space— thundered into the Earth's surface. It may have weighed as much as 885,000 tons and measured 330 feet in diameter. The impact was such that the force threw up a bank around the crater 130 feet above the level of the surrounding desert.

Most meteorites burn or break up as they meet the resistance of the Earth's atmosphere. Scientists believe that this one was so vast, and moving at such high speed, that it hardly slowed down in the atmosphere and reached the Earth in one piece. It exploded on impact, scattering fragments of rock over a large area. Many of these fragments have been found and identified, but excavations in the crater itself have revealed no large mass that could have been part of the meteorite. The scientists' estimate of its size is calculated from the size of the crater.

▲ The typical shape of the Barringer Crater, with its deep center and slightly raised edges, is visible from the air above the Arizona desert.

The Barringer Crater is only about 60 miles from Holbrook, Arizona, where another amazing meteorite strike occurred on July 19, 1912. Local people were astounded to find small stones raining from the sky. A total of 14,000 stones was eventually counted.

◀ Like part of the landscape of the Moon, the Barringer Crater is enormous. But there is no sign of the vast meteorite that made it some 50,000 years ago.

The plagues of Egypt

c. 1300 BC

The Old Testament book of Exodus tells of nine plagues that struck Ancient Egypt while the Israelites were slaves there. In the Exodus story, the plagues were God's warning to Pharaoh that Moses must be allowed to lead the Israelites out of Egypt.

The Ancient Egyptians relied on the Nile, and the first plague—pollution, which killed the fish in the river—would have been a serious blow. But there was worse to come. Frogs, driven from the river by the rotting fish, invaded homes, while gnats and flies bred on the dead fish. The flies carried disease to cattle and skin infections to humans. Next, hail and storms ruined the crops, and the wind brought a swarm of locusts, which devoured the remaining vegetation. Finally, for three days the sky turned dark, probably because of a duststorm.

▲ This early illustration shows the hail and storms described in Exodus, the only source of the story. Other plagues might naturally have followed a long period of unusually violent weather.

The annual flooding of the Nile delta provided Egypt with rich soil for centuries, but as towns and cities on the delta grew, it became difficult to cope with. In 1970, the Aswan High Dam was built at the head of the lower valley. This provided hydroelectric power for Egypt and also ended the annual floods.

▼ This illustration from an early German Bible shows the plague of flies, which killed all the cattle.

L'Aigle meteorite shower
1803

On April 26, 1803, the people of L'Aigle in northeastern France, about 100 miles west of Paris, were startled by a storm that swept across the village. But this was no ordinary storm. It was a shower of meteorites, which poured down along an 8-mile track.

Over 2,300 stones rained down on the village. Each weighed between a quarter ounce and 20 lb. No one was killed or injured, but it was a terrifying experience for the villagers. The shower occurred in daylight, and there were many witnesses. Some said that before it started they heard loud explosions and saw brilliant lights in the sky. Others, who had picked up the stones, reported that they were still hot.

A French physicist, Jean Baptiste Biot (1774–1862), carried out an investigation. He analyzed some of the stones to find out what they were made of. He confirmed they were solid material from outer space. Until then, scientists had doubted stories about stones from space.

▼ A meteor track crosses the night sky. Its bright line is caused by glowing trails of dust particles which glow as they travel through the Earth's atmosphere.

Since the L'Aigle incident, showers of meteorites have been reported from other places. The largest on record was near Holbrook in Arizona on July 19, 1912. Most of the stones were very small and looked like grape seeds. Each stone formed a black crust as it burned its way through the atmosphere.

Tunguska fireball
1908

No one knows exactly what happened in the sky over the Tunguska region of Siberia at dawn on June 30, 1908, but it caused a major explosion with the force of a nuclear bomb. It was the most destructive natural event of its kind in modern times. No one saw it happen, and the explosion left no crater. The Tunguska region, in central Siberia near the Arctic Circle, is almost uninhabited and there were no human casualties, although many reindeer were killed.

The most likely explanation is that the Tunguska fireball was caused by a small comet, which, entering the Earth's atmosphere, blew apart high above the Earth's surface. The force of the explosion shattered the comet's solid matter into tiny fragments. Some of these were later recovered from the soil. There was huge damage to the forests in the area. Thousands of trees were stripped of their foliage and flattened for

▲ In the bleak landscape of central Siberia the explosion of the Tunguska fireball brought destruction only to reindeer and trees.

several miles in all directions. The effects of the destruction caused by the fireball can still be seen today.

It was sheer good luck that the explosion took place where it did. A similar event over a densely populated area would have brought instant death to thousands of people.

A similar but less violent event took place, also in Siberia, in 1947. A meteorite, which entered the atmosphere near Vladivostok, also exploded in midair. Large pieces of rock were embedded in the earth and later analyzed by scientists.

The Antioch earthquake

AD 526

Antioch, in what is now Turkey, was once the greatest trading center of the Byzantine Empire, a rich and splendid city. On May 29, 526, it was bustling with visitors who had come to celebrate the Feast of the Ascension. Most people were having their evening meal when, just after 6 p.m., a huge shock brought Antioch's buildings—its fine churches and palaces, as well as its humble homes—crashing to the ground. The first tremor was followed by aftershocks that did further damage and, to complete Antioch's night of horror, fire broke out. "Fire fell from heaven instead of rain," one observer wrote.

Almost all the city's buildings were destroyed. The golden-domed Great Church, the city's pride, survived the initial shock only to catch fire and collapse five days later. Between 250,000 and 300,000 people lost their lives. As the survivors staggered about among the ruins, bandits moved into the city to rob and murder them, and loot their homes. Aftershocks continued in Antioch for another eighteen months.

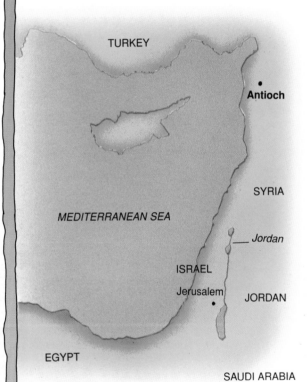

TURKEY

Antioch

SYRIA

MEDITERRANEAN SEA

Jordan

ISRAEL

Jerusalem   JORDAN

EGYPT

SAUDI ARABIA

The rebuilding of Antioch began when the aftershocks had passed, but not for long. Another earthquake in November 528 brought the work to a halt. From then on, the reign of Antioch as the chief trading center of the Byzantine Empire was over.

◀ This woodcut of the Antioch earthquake was made hundreds of years after the event, but it gives some impression of the total destruction that the disaster brought to the city.

Shensi Province earthquake
1556

The greatest natural disaster in human history, in terms of the number of lives lost, occurred in Shensi Province in northwestern China in 1556. Shensi Province is bounded to the south by the Yellow River and to the north by the Great Wall. At that time Shensi's main city, Xian, was the capital of China and, with over one million inhabitants, was the largest city in the world.

Disaster struck without warning at night. A huge earthquake, which was felt over half the land area of China, shook the region. Thousands of people were killed outright as their flimsy timber homes collapsed around them. Fires, started by debris falling onto hearths, raged through the ruins. Many Shensi people who lived in caves hollowed out of soft cliffs died when the cliffs caved in. Many people were buried by landslides or carried away by floods. Some small villages simply disappeared, swallowed up by the huge tremor or its consequences. The number of deaths was estimated as 830,000.

MONGOLIA

Beijing

N. KOREA

S. KOREA

SHENSI PROVINCE

Shanghai

TAIWAN

Hong Kong

CHINA SEA

MYANMAR (BURMA)

THAILAND

BAY OF BENGAL

There have been nine earthquakes in recorded history that have each killed more than 100,000 people. Six of these occurred in China, two in Japan and one in India.

◀ China is shown on this seventeenth-century map. The earthquake was felt throughout the country, and it took years before Shensi returned to normal life.

The Lisbon earthquake
1755

On November 1, 1755, a huge shock was felt across the whole of Europe. It was so powerful that the waters of inland lakes up to 1,750 miles away rose and fell in time with the shock waves the quake created. But this was nothing compared with the destruction the earthquake caused near its center.

The Portuguese city of Lisbon was a prosperous port and trading center. The earthquake's centre was beneath the Atlantic Ocean to the west. There had been no warning of disaster when the people of Lisbon felt three huge shocks, one after the other. The city's buildings were shattered and fires started, adding to the damage and loss of life.

Worse was to come. The shock waves under the sea set up a tsunami, or tidal wave, that wrecked ships in the harbor and flooded the city.

▲ Few of the tall, elegant buildings of the Portuguese city of Lisbon stood a chance of survival in the great earthquake of 1755. Many people lost their lives as the buildings tumbled down.

The Lisbon earthquake inspired an English geologist, John Michell, to make the first-ever study of earthquakes. He realized that they are caused by shock waves moving through the Earth's crust. Michell was the founder of seismology, the branch of geology concerned with earthquakes.

▼ Probably most of the 60,000 victims of the Lisbon earthquake drowned in the enormous tidal wave that followed it.

The New Madrid earthquake
1811

In December 1811, the people of the small town of New Madrid, Missouri, were looking forward to Christmas and the New Year. Little did they know that they were on the brink of a season of terror.

On December 16, the first of a series of earthquakes struck the little town. New Madrid was not in an area known to be at risk from earthquakes, and no one living there had ever experienced anything like it before. The shock was so great that it was felt right across North America. The vibrations caused church bells to ring in Washington DC, 625 miles away. But there was no time for the people of New Madrid to recover from the first shock before more followed. One of these later shocks changed the course of the nearby Mississippi River in several places.

The earthquakes continued at frequent intervals until February 1812. By that time, New Madrid's wooden houses had been reduced to splinters.

The population, fearing that the shocks would go on for ever, fled from the town. Many families settled elsewhere and never returned. The New Madrid earthquake was probably the most severe ever recorded in North America.

▼ This nineteenth-century map of the lower Mississippi River shows New Madrid and the area that was most badly affected by the earthquake that changed the course of one of America's great rivers.

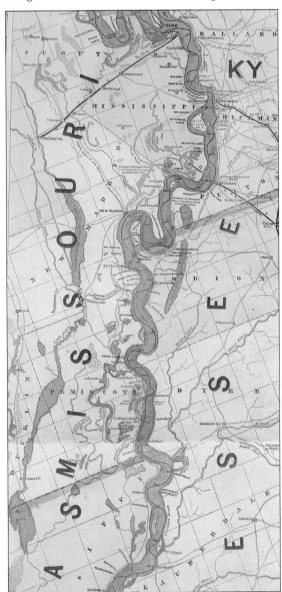

Earthquakes kill an average of 15,000 people each year and do millions of dollars' worth of damage. It has been estimated that 100 million people have died in earthquakes in the history of humankind.

The San Francisco earthquake

1906

The Pacific coast of California runs parallel to a series of cracks in the Earth's crust which are called "faults." These have caused many earthquakes over the years, but none as severe as the tremor that struck the city of San Francisco at dawn on April 18, 1906.

Although minor aftershocks occurred during the weeks that followed the San Francisco earthquake, the main shock lasted for less than one minute. But in that minute, gas mains and electricity cables were broken, causing large fires in the city center. The majority of the 700 people who died were victims of the fires rather than of the earthquake itself. Rescue workers had to demolish buildings around the fire to create gaps too wide for the flames to cross. Buildings in an area of over 4 sq. miles were destroyed.

The people of California live in constant fear of another major earthquake. Research shows that one can be expected every fifty to a hundred years. Schools and hospitals hold regular earthquake drills, and emergency services constantly practice the skills they will need when the Earth trembles again.

▼ Earthquakes cannot be prevented, but the lessons of 1906 helped architects to design better, more earthquake-proof buildings.

Valparaiso earthquake
1906

Valparaiso is on the Pacific coast of Chile, in one of the areas of the world most prone to earthquakes. It was built on slopes that fall steeply to the sea. The city had been shaken by severe tremors many times in its history—in 1731, 1822, 1839 and 1873—but the most devastating earthquake to strike Valparaiso occurred on August 16, 1906.

That night there was an unusually violent thunderstorm. Soon afterwards, the earthquake struck. Two-thirds of the city was destroyed in an upheaval that raised the coastline by over 3 feet and changed the shape of the slopes on which most of Valparaiso's homes were built. There were 1,500 deaths, and most of the population was made homeless. Afterwards there was an outbreak of looting, and the government was forced to impose martial law to regain control.

Apart from earthquakes, Valparaiso has suffered more than its fair share of destruction since the city was founded in 1536. The English captured it twice. The Dutch plundered it in 1600, and the Spanish in 1866. In 1891, it was laid to waste during the Chilean civil war.

▼ The business district along the waterfront of the Bay of Valparaiso was almost completely wrecked.

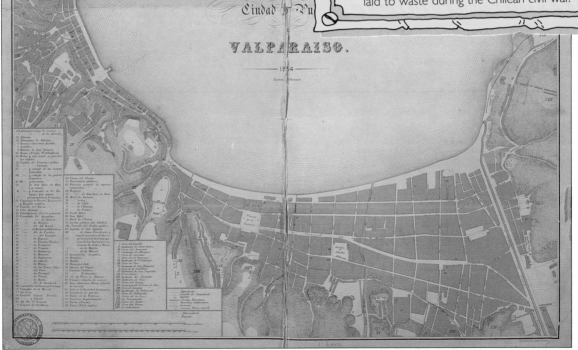

Messina earthquake
1908

Messina is the second largest city in Sicily, on the northeastern tip of the island facing the Italian mainland across the Straits of Messina. It was famous for its beauty until the disastrous events of December 28, 1908.

Early in the morning, Messina was shaken by the worst earthquake ever recorded in Europe. The shock, which originated under the sea, spread destruction throughout the countryside surrounding the city and across the Straits of Messina on the southern tip of the mainland. At Messina, and in the port of Reggio on the mainland, the land subsided by over two feet.

The two cities were destroyed, and in Messina about 75,000 people—half the population—died. A further 75,000 died in the ruined villages of the Sicilian countryside and on the mainland.

▼ Emergency surgical stations were set up to try to save some of the victims of the earthquake.

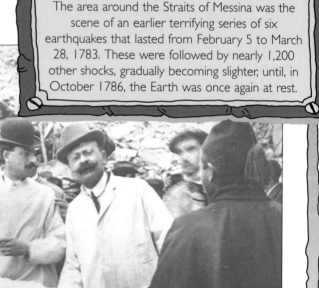

The area around the Straits of Messina was the scene of an earlier terrifying series of six earthquakes that lasted from February 5 to March 28, 1783. These were followed by nearly 1,200 other shocks, gradually becoming slighter, until, in October 1786, the Earth was once again at rest.

Kanto earthquake
1923

At about midday on September 1, 1923, there was an earthquake beneath Sagami Bay, on Japan's main island of Honshu. Within minutes many buildings in the cities of Tokyo and Yokohama, about 50 miles to the north, lay in ruins.

In Tokyo, families were cooking their meals on traditional charcoal braziers. These were overturned by the tremors, starting fires that spread through the city's wooden houses. Families fled in panic, and then found themselves trapped between a wall of flames and the Sumida River. Hundreds of people were drowned as the spreading fires forced them into the water.

Then came the second blow—a tsunami (or tidal wave) sweeping in from the sea. Almost 700,000 homes were destroyed or seriously damaged. The death toll reached 130,000.

▼ On September 3, people were clearing debris from the streets even though aftershocks were still being felt. It was Japan's worst ever earthquake.

The Kanto earthquake alerted Japanese engineers and architects to the need to design earthquake-proof buildings. Their success was shown in 1987 when a major earthquake that struck Tokyo resulted in only two deaths and 53 injuries.

Anchorage earthquake
1964

Good Friday, March 27, 1964, was a fine, sunny day in Anchorage, Alaska's largest city. The people of the city were enjoying their holiday picnicking in the country or sailing off the coast. Many were still out of town when, at about 5:30 p.m., Anchorage was rocked by a huge earthquake centered some 80 miles to the east of the city in Prince William Sound. The tremor continued for four minutes. The city's main street was split in two by a crack nearly 20 inches wide. One side dropped by about 20 feet. Along the southern coast of Alaska, cliffs slid into the sea.

The shock was followed by a tsunami, or tidal wave, that carried boats far inland. Yet, amazingly, the death toll was only 131, far fewer than might have been expected after such a destructive shock and flood.

Alaska forms part of the "Pacific rim," where the Earth's crust is most unstable, and is liable to sudden volcanic outbursts. In 1912, Mount Katmai, previously quiet, suddenly exploded, and blew off its top. The area is now a national park.

◀ Because of the holiday, few people were out on the streets when the earthquake struck. But in spite of the low number of casualties, the damage to the economy of Anchorage and Alaska was devastating.

Tangshan earthquake
1976

Tangshan, with a population of over six million, is an industrial city in northern China. On July 28, 1976, the city and the surrounding province were rocked by a violent earthquake that shook buildings in China's capital, Beijing, 100 miles away. It was China's worst earthquake for twelve years.

Among many miraculous escapes was that of a woman who got out of her hotel in the city only two seconds before it split in two and crumbled to the ground. Most of Tangshan's population took to the roads out of the city, fearing further shocks. Makeshift camps were set up outside to give them shelter.

The true death toll from the quake will probably never be known. The official number of dead was put at 142,000, but Western experts believe that the figure was much higher—perhaps as high as 650,000. If this is true, Tangshan was China's second most destructive earthquake, in terms of loss of life.

▼ The damage to this coastal railway shows the sort of destruction that occurred at Tangshan.

Earthquakes are caused by movements of the plates that make up the Earth's crust. Many of these movements take place at the eastern and western edges of the Pacific Ocean, which explains why China, Japan and the western coasts of North and South America are so vulnerable to earthquakes.

The Armenian earthquake

1988

Few earthquakes have caused as much destruction as the huge tremor that shook Armenia in southern Russia at 11:41 in the morning of December 7, 1988. The town of Spivak was completely flattened and most of the 20,000 people who lived there killed. In Armenia's largest city, Leninakan, 30 miles from the center of the earthquake, four out of every five buildings were destroyed, and in nearby Kirovakan almost every building collapsed.

The earthquake caused severe damage across about 3,975 sq. miles of countryside. The official death toll was 55,000, but other estimates put the number of dead closer to 100,000. Half a million families were made homeless.

Armenia was completely unprepared for the disaster. Buildings collapsed like

houses of cards. There was no decent rescue equipment. Until machinery arrived from outside, rescue workers worked with their bare hands.

> When the Armenian earthquake struck, Mikhail Gorbachev, newly elected president of the then Soviet Union, of which Armenia was part, was on a visit to the United States. He immediately canceled his trip and returned to take personal charge of the rescue effort.

▼ Their homes destroyed, people had to warm themselves by fires made in the open air.

Kobe earthquake
1995

The Kobe earthquake was a disaster that everyone thought could not happen. Japan's second largest port, Kobe, had been rebuilt after bombing during World War II, and its buildings, bridges and roads were said to be earthquake proof.

At 5:46 on the morning of January 17, 1995, the people of Kobe discovered how untrue those claims were. A severe earthquake shook the city, reducing thousands of buildings to rubble and seriously damaging thousands more. Kobe's road and rail links were broken and twisted. Over 5,000 people died, 27,000 were injured and 370,000 made homeless in the earthquake and the fires that followed.

The emergency services were overwhelmed. Rescue efforts were hampered by the lack of electricity and the pall of smoke that hung over the ruins. In the days following the tremor, there were frequent aftershocks, striking

▲ Damage to roads like this expressway hampered the emergency services in Kobe. The destruction of water mains made it impossible for fire-fighting equipment to be used in many areas.

new terror into survivors. Thousands of people had to shelter in tents as the temperature dropped below freezing.

Kobe would take years to rebuild, but experiences there have forced the world take a new look at the destructive power of earthquakes.

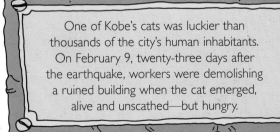

One of Kobe's cats was luckier than thousands of the city's human inhabitants. On February 9, twenty-three days after the earthquake, workers were demolishing a ruined building when the cat emerged, alive and unscathed—but hungry.

◄ Great columns of smoke could be seen rising from the buildings of Kobe as the aftershocks of the earthquake continued.

The devastation of Knossos

c. 1450 BC

Between 2000 and 1450 BC, the palace of Knossos on the Mediterranean island of Crete was the center of the Minoan civilization. Santorini is a volcanic island about 68 miles north of the island of Crete.

In about 1450 BC, there were devastating geological disturbances in Santorini and in Crete. It is not known whether these disturbances occurred a few years apart or all at the same time. However, a huge volcanic explosion on Santorini was followed by a tidal wave. The settlements on Santorini were totally destroyed by rivers of molten rock. Meanwhile, a great cloud of volcanic ash rose into the air and, according to some archaeologists, buried the palace of Knossos.

Certainly, when Knossos was excavated in the early years of the twentieth century, the archaeologists had to dig through volcanic material. They also discovered severe earthquake damage, which may possibly have been caused by the same disturbance.

One theory is that the earthquake may have happened first, giving the Minoans time to abandon Knossos and take to their boats. They may then have been overwhelmed by the tidal wave. The exact sequence of events will never be known, but the disasters marked the beginning of the end for the Minoan civilization.

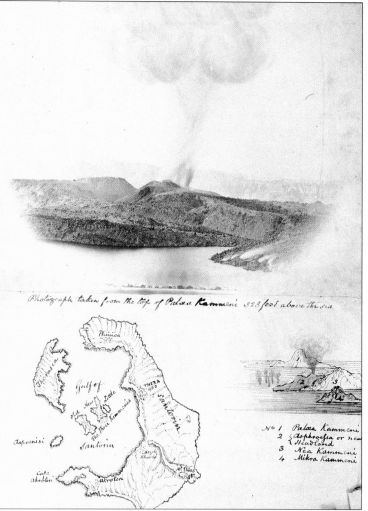

▲ The island of Santorini, north of Crete, is shown here in sketches and a photograph. The ash from the island's volcanic eruptions is thought to have completely buried the great palace of Knossos.

Santorini has continued throughout history to be the scene of violent eruptions. The most spectacular of these was an underwater explosion in 196 BC, when for four days flames leaped from the sea. At the end of this time, a new island had been formed.

The destruction of Pompeii

AD 79

Vesuvius is a volcano in southern Italy overlooking the Bay of Naples. Near its foot, the ancient Romans built the towns of Pompeii, Herculaneum and Stabiae. The Romans had no reason to fear living close to Vesuvius or farming its slopes. It had never erupted before.

At about noon on August 24, AD 79, without warning, Vesuvius exploded. A hail of ash and pebbles spouted from it and covered Pompeii in a layer of ash nearly 13 feet deep. Herculaneum, to the north, was engulfed by a river of mud and volcanic debris. Stabiae, on the coast, suffered a similar fate.

For many people, there was no time to escape. They were buried alive as they worked. Some managed to shelter in cellars, but there was no escape from the suffocating blanket of lava and ash. Many who were not trapped inside the buildings were killed by the choking, poisonous fumes that filled the air. No one knows how many people died, but 2,000 skeletons have been discovered in Pompeii alone.

Pompeii and Herculaneum lay buried until, about 250 years ago, archaeologists began to uncover their ruins.

▲ Layers of volcanic ash preserved the remains of Pompeii in near-perfect condition. Much of what we know about life in Roman times is based on the remains found at Pompeii.

Vesuvius, often seen with a plume of smoke above it, is still an active volcano today. It erupts frequently, sometimes severely enough to put at risk the people who continue to live in the villages below.

▼ This painting by eighteenth-century French artist Jacques Antoine Volaire gives a powerful impression of what an eruption of Vesuvius can be like, with a sea of red-hot lava and palls of thick smoke.

Mount Etna eruption
1669

Mount Etna stands 10,958 feet high on the eastern coast of Sicily. It is an active volcano that has erupted frequently.

The worst eruption began on the night of Friday March 8, 1669. An earthquake tremor was followed by roarings from inside the mountain. On the following Monday there were three violent explosions, and boulders weighing up to 300 lbs were hurled several miles into the air. A rain of red-hot cinders fell on the surrounding country, destroying several villages.

It was found that a crack nearly 5 feet wide and 10 miles long had opened in the side of Mount Etna. A river of lava (molten rock) emerged from the crack and flowed down toward the nearby city of Calabria. Officially, 20,000 people were killed, but other estimates put the total as high as 100,000.

▲ This flow of lava from Etna was photographed during the eruption in 1979. In 1669, the lava destroyed much of the city of Calabria, 17 miles from the summit.

The Ancient Romans believed that the rumblings and eruptions of Mount Etna were expressions of anger by their god of fire, Vulcan. This is how the word "volcano" entered the language.

◄ A satellite photograph of Mount Etna shows one flank of the summit covered with snow, while a plume of smoke and steam from the volcano stretches in the opposite direction.

Laki eruption
1783

Iceland is a land of volcanoes. There are well over a hundred on the island, of which twenty-five have erupted in fairly recent times. One of the most disastrous eruptions occurred in 1783. Laki, a volcano in the south of the island that had previously been dormant, suddenly came to life. It sent clouds of ash into the air, and at the same time a river of lava flowed out of the volcano along a path 20 miles wide, covering 218 sq. miles.

Laki is in a remote spot in the mountains well away from any settlements, and there were no immediate casualties. But within hours of the eruption Icelanders realized that a major disaster was looming. A rain of volcanic ash began to descend all over the island, covering the ground and smothering vegetation. Crops were ruined. Pasture was destroyed, and 11,500 cattle, 28,000 horses and 190,500 sheep starved to death.

The following winter was grim for the Icelanders. They ate through their stores of food, and famine set in. One-fifth of the island's population, about 9,500 people, died of hunger.

BAFFIN ISLAND

GREENLAND

Arctic Circle

Reykjavic

NORWAY

ICELAND

NORTH ATLANTIC OCEAN

UNITED KINGDOM

London

In 1963, volcanic activity under the sea off Iceland's southwestern coast created a new island. The crew of a fishing boat noticed that the sea seemed to be boiling. Within twenty-four hours a new volcanic island had appeared. It was named Surtsey.

The Tambora explosion

1815

No one in the world escaped the effects of the violent eruption of the Tambora volcano on an island east of Java in what is now Indonesia. The explosion in April 1815 altered climatic conditions all over the world for over a year.

The eruption blew an estimated 1.67 million tons of ash and rocks into the air. When the smoke had cleared, it could be seen that Tambora had "blown its top," reducing its height from 13,451 feet to 9,350 feet. The explosion was heard 1,550 miles away.

About 10,000 islanders were killed immediately. The eruption was followed by a tsunami (tidal wave), which along with the disease and famine that followed, killed a further 82,000.

Meanwhile, some of the ash from Tambora formed a layer in the Earth's atmosphere. This blocked the heat and light of the Sun all over the Earth. The result was a period of very wet weather, snow tinged with red, blue and brown dust, and brightly colored sunsets.

▲ Material thrown up by a volcano can affect the weather. In 1816, the effects lasted so long that it was known as "the year without summer."

The landscape paintings of J.M.W. Turner (1775–1851) are renowned for their vivid use of color. In 1815, he was starting the series of paintings that brought him fame. It is thought that the remarkable skies in his paintings portrayed the effects of the Tambora eruption on the atmosphere.

▶ This view of Tambora was taken from the Space Shuttle. It shows the caldera (the crater at the top of the volcano), which is some 4 miles across.

Krakatoa

1883

Krakatoa in Indonesia is a volcanic island of 5 sq. miles. In the spring of 1883, it began to rumble and throw out showers of ashes and stones, but this was not unusual and few people took any notice. Then, on August 26, the noise grew louder and the showers of hot material more threatening. Two days later, Krakatoa blew itself apart in a massive explosion that destroyed more than two-thirds of the island.

The island was uninhabited, and the eruption itself caused no loss of life. But it had terrible consequences. The volcano's explosions and collapse set up a tsunami (tidal wave) 115 feet high that engulfed nearby inhabited islands and the shores of the Sunda Strait on Java and Sumatra. Further waves poured over the shattered sea walls. More than 36,000 people were drowned. The ashes from the explosion at Krakatoa shot high into the atmosphere, darkening the skies over the whole of Indonesia and coloring sunsets all over the world.

The explosion at Krakatoa made the loudest sound in human history. The bang was heard in parts of Western and South Australia up to 2,250 miles from the volcano, and even on the Indian Ocean island of Rodriguez 2,983 miles away.

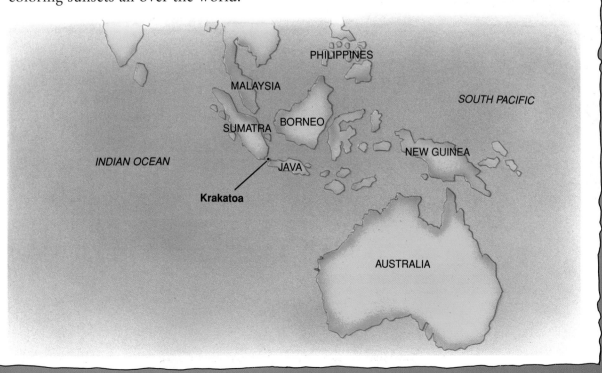

Mount Pelée
1902

The eruption of Mount Pelée on the island of Martinique in the Caribbean caused the greatest ever death toll from a volcano. Mount Pelée, 4,430 feet high, stands in the north of the island. The town of St Pierre lay about 5 miles away.

Signs of trouble came in April 1902, when showers of ash from Mount Pelée fell on the surrounding area. A week later, about 150 people were killed when lava (molten rock) from the volcano flowed through sugar plantations near St Pierre. Then on May 8, Mount Pelée erupted violently, sending a river of lava down through St Pierre and killing some 40,000 people.

Damage to the economy of Martinique was so great, and the loss of life so shocking, that immediately after the eruption of Mount Pelée it was planned to evacuate the island completely. Instead, the economy was rebuilt, and today Martinique has a population of 327,000, nearly twice the number before the eruption.

▲ Showers of ash and lava, together with poisonous fumes from the volcano, killed many. Even more died in the resulting fires in St Pierre.

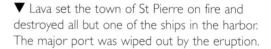

▼ Lava set the town of St Pierre on fire and destroyed all but one of the ships in the harbor. The major port was wiped out by the eruption.

Mount St Helens
1980

Mount St Helens, in Washington, was a familiar tourist landmark. Its conical shape, with distinctive snow-covered peak, rose from a beautiful forest landscape. On May 18, 1980, it changed its appearance forever.

An eruption had been expected. For months there had been rumblings from the volcano, and small clouds of steam and ash were seen above it from time to time. But no one expected that the eruption would be so catastrophic.

When the main explosion came, it tore off the top of the mountain, leaving a huge, gaping hole. Clouds of burning ash and poisonous gas swept across the landscape, destroying everything in their path. The ice at the peak of the volcano melted, carrying rocks, mud and water into the valleys below. The area of destruction stretched 20 miles.

The height of the mountain was reduced from 9,678 feet before the eruption to its present height of 8,399 feet. The floods tore down bridges and swept away buildings. But miraculously, only sixty-three people died.

▲ Ash, hot gases and fragments of rock shoot out of Mount St Helens during its eruption in 1980.

The Mount St Helens area has now become a National Volcanic Monument, with a special access road for tourists. The United States government also uses the site to educate people about the danger of volcanic eruptions.

▼ This infrared photograph shows the volcanic ash in pink and red; it indicates how far the ash spread: 232 sq. miles of forest were destroyed.

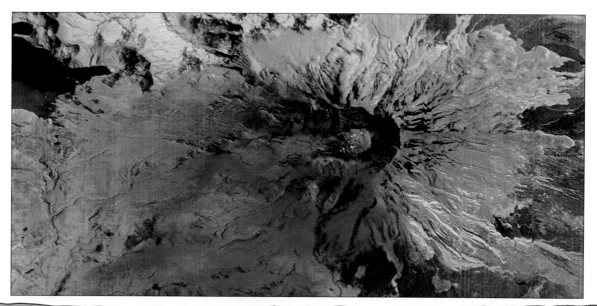

Armero
1985

Even if volcanoes erupt in uninhabited areas, they often produce aftereffects that threaten lives some distance away. This is what happened when the Nevado del Ruiz volcano, in Colombia, high in the Andes Mountains, erupted.

No one lives near Nevado del Ruiz, but about 30 miles away was the town of Armero. It lay in the valley of the La Lagunilla River, which is fed by streams that run down from the volcano.

Nevado del Ruiz erupted late one afternoon in 1985, shooting ash 26,246 feet into the air. The first sign of the disaster to come was the ash that started to rain on the streets of Armero. As darkness fell, a torrent of mud cascaded down from the volcano, swept along by overflowing streams and rivers. A few people had time to clamber onto their roofs. But for 20,000 out of Armero's 23,000 population, there was no time to escape. The mud flooded into the town, burying them and their houses.

It was all over in little more than 15 minutes. Rescuers flying over the town the next morning reported that it was as if Armero had never existed.

▲ A plume of smoke rises high into the air above Nevado del Ruiz, the volcano that destroyed the town of Armero, Colombia.

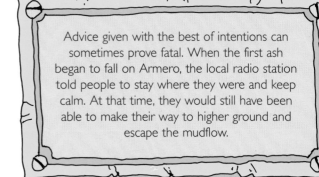

Advice given with the best of intentions can sometimes prove fatal. When the first ash began to fall on Armero, the local radio station told people to stay where they were and keep calm. At that time, they would still have been able to make their way to higher ground and escape the mudflow.

▼ Mud from the volcano laid waste even the largest buildings in Armero after the eruption in 1985.

The Great Flood

c. 6000 BC

The legends of many of the world's cultures include the story of a great flood, which is thought to have happened about 8,000 years ago, or possibly even earlier. The Old Testament of the Bible has the story of Noah's flood, during which Noah saved two of each species in the Ark.

Similar stories of a flood disaster appear in the 5,000-year-old *Epic of Gilgamesh*, written on clay tablets by the ancient Assyrians, in the legends of the native peoples of North and South America, and in the traditional stories of the people of Hawaii and China.

These stories are all so similar that experts believe that they are all accounts of the same flood that overwhelmed the world at some time before 5000 BC. Some of the legends tell of fierce storms, ships being marooned (like Noah's ark)

▲ This Islamic illustration of the story of the flood, showing Noah in his ark, comes from a manuscript written down in the late sixteenth century.

One of the stories of the Great Flood comes from a clay tablet that was in the library of King Ashurbanipal I of Assyria, who reigned from 669 to 626 BC. The tablet was discovered in pieces in 1872 by a British archaeologist. He reassembled it and found it contained part of a story very similar to the biblical story of Noah.

on the peaks of mountains, cities being swept into the sea and people fleeing for survival to caves high in the mountains.

We will never know any of the details of the Great Flood, but it seems likely that there was a great natural catastrophe —or perhaps several. The memories of this event were preserved by ancient peoples in their legends, which have survived to the present day as part of our culture and literature.

◄ The animals leave Noah's ark after the flood waters start to go down in this picture from a fifteenth-century English book of hours.

Huang He floods

1887, 1931 and 1938

The Huang He, or Yellow River, flows for about 3,000 miles in a great S-bend through northern China. For the last quarter of its course it flows across a low-lying, fertile plain where millions of Chinese people live.

Huang He is sometimes called "China's sorrow" because of the floods, which have often destroyed so many lives and communities along its lower banks. For over 4,000 years the Chinese have been trying to protect these communities by building dikes and cutting channels to take flood water away. But the Huang He has continued to flood at frequent intervals. In 1887, up to two million Chinese died when the Huang He flooded. In the floods of 1931, three million were killed, and in 1938, some 500,000 were drowned.

MONGOLIA

Beijing

Huang He   Shanghai

CHINA

Hong Kong

CHINA SEA

MYANMAR
(BURMA)

LAOS

THAILAND

BAY OF BENGAL

The Yellow River takes its name from the yellow earth carried in the water from the upper reaches of the river. As the current slows down on the lower plain, this earth sinks to the river bed, raising the level of the water and thereby increasing the risk of flooding.

▲ The powerful flood waters of the Huang He can sometimes sweep away entire buildings.

▶ A makeshift bridge allows people to cross the flooded area on the plain near the Huang He.

North Sea floods
1953

On January 31, 1953, a fierce storm, with northwesterly winds reaching 127 mph, swept across the North Sea between Britain and western Europe. It was also the day of a high spring tide. The two factors combined to create a "surge"—a wall of water that battered the North Sea coast.

The low-lying coastal areas of eastern England, northern Belgium and the southern Netherlands—many of which were below sea level—had dikes or banks to protect them, but the sea burst through the banks or flowed over them. The disaster was sudden, and there was no time for people to escape.

In Belgium and the Netherlands over 1,800 people drowned. Over 300 lives were lost in England. Thousands of families were made homeless. Many animals were drowned, and the saltwater made land unusable for growing crops for years afterward. Only the turning of the tide stopped water flooding from the River Thames into central London, which could have cost thousands more lives.

▲ On the low-lying Canvey Island, England, houses were almost completely submerged and people had to be evacuated.

Surface drainage, as well as irrigation from underground water, can cause subsidence. Some parts of the Fens in eastern England have fallen by as much as 13 feet over the past century. The cutting of drainage channels has caused the peat soil to dry out and sink.

◄ The flood waters were too strong for many buildings, which were simply pushed bodily from their foundations. This photograph was taken two days after the surge, when the water level had begun to drop.

The Mississippi floods
1993

The Mississippi River forms a great flood plain as it meanders its way in huge loops toward the Gulf of Mexico. It flows slowly, depositing layers of mud from further upstream. Americans call the river "the Big Muddy." Its delta is the outlet into the sea for water from a vast area between the Rocky Mountains and the Appalachian Mountains.

Flooding has always been a problem on this low-lying land. In 1717, the first levees, or dikes, were built to contain the river waters, and there are now over 2,000 miles of these flood defenses. Yet the waters of the Mississippi still flood from time to time.

In July 1993, the Mississippi region experienced its worst flooding for 150 years. The river, swollen by heavy rainfall, either burst open or overflowed more than two-thirds of the levees. At least fifty people were killed and 70,000 made homeless. Water covered 17,000 sq. miles of land. The flooding started on July 4, but it was not until August 10 that the waters began to recede and the people of the lower Mississippi could begin to rebuild their lives.

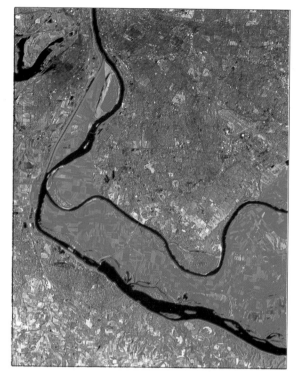

▲ This false-color satellite photograph of the Mississippi River was taken during July 1993. The red shows the area covered by the flood waters.

The combination of floods and storms can bring sudden disaster to the Mississippi plain. During a flood in 1927, residents of Arkansas City reported that the streets had been dry at midday, but two hours later mules were drowning before they could be unhitched from their carts.

LEFT TO
BROADWAY

The Great Storm
1703

On November 26, 1703, people in Britain were awakened by unusually strong winds. They expected that the storm would soon "blow itself out"—but it went on "with a strange and unusual violence," as one eyewitness wrote.

The Great Storm raged all that day across southern Britain. It tore through cities and countryside, uprooting trees, toppling church steeples, flattening houses, causing havoc on both land and sea. Off the Devon coast, the Eddystone lighthouse, towering 121 feet above the water, was swept away, drowning the keepers and the lighthouse's builder, Henry Winstanley. Over 8,000 other people died, mostly crushed in the wreckage of their homes.

So many buildings were wrecked in London and Bristol that the two cities looked like battlefields. In the county of Kent alone, 17,000 trees were brought down. In Sussex, flood waters had broken through the banks of the River Ouse, moving its mouth 1 mile along the coast to the west.

A detailed eyewitness account of the Great Storm was written by the author, journalist and traveler Daniel Defoe. He later became better known for his story *Robinson Crusoe*, based on the real-life adventures of a shipwrecked sailor.

▼ This nineteenth-century painting conjures up the windswept atmosphere on the night of the storm.

Calcutta cyclone

1737

Meteorologists use the word "cyclone" to describe any weather system in which winds revolve around a low-pressure area. But in the Indian subcontinent "cyclone" has a special meaning. It describes a violent storm with a low-pressure area at its center. In other parts of the world this kind of storm is called a hurricane or a typhoon.

In 1737, a cyclone struck the Indian city of Calcutta. Built on the banks of the Hugli River, Calcutta was then India's largest city. Sprawling and badly planned, it stretched along the lower reaches of the river, which are affected by the tides in the Bay of Bengal. Many of the houses were built below the high-tide water level.

When the cyclone swept in from the Bay of Bengal, the winds reached over 125 mph. The sea, whipped up by the fierce winds into a great wave, drove inland along the river, flooding thousands of homes. Many people who managed to escape from their houses were drowned in the floodwater outside. Others were simply overwhelmed in the places where they worked.

It will never be known exactly how many people were killed, but the death toll has been estimated as 300,000.

▲ A modern photograph of flooding on the plains of India shows what the aftereffects of the cyclone must have looked like in the countryside outside the city.

Calcutta and Bangladesh to the east have been devastated by cyclones many times. In 1864, 48,000 people died, and there was an even worse cyclone twelve years later, resulting in 100,000 deaths. You can read about the cyclones that have devasted Bangladesh on pages 42 and 46.

▶ Swirling cyclone clouds, with a central dark hole ("the eye of the storm") were visible from a Russian spacecraft in 1978.

Galveston hurricane
1900

The worst hurricane in American history struck the Texas city of Galveston on September 8, 1900. The city is on an island, connected to the mainland by a causeway 2 miles long. The storm moved across the Gulf of Mexico, with winds up to 135 mph driving waves 23 feet high in front of them. Unwisely, many of the citizens of Galveston went down to the shore to watch. Thousands were overwhelmed before they had time to escape. A total of 6,000 lives were lost. The storm raged for eighteen hours before moving further north and dying away.

The city was devastated. Survivors of the storm began to die of hunger and thirst, and the U.S. Army was called in to provide food and tents. There was widespread looting and the Army had to take drastic measures to maintain law and order. Twenty-five of the looters were shot dead.

▲ The strength of the storm-driven waves was such that even large buildings, like this church, could not stand their force.

When Galveston was rebuilt, the land was raised about 15 feet above the previous level. The city was protected by a new sea wall that was higher than the storm's high-water mark and over 6 feet above the previous high-water record.

◄ The beach area at Galveston was totally devastated, and many of the wooden houses were overturned.

Bangladesh cyclone
1970

Bangladesh is occupied almost entirely by the low-lying deltas of three rivers, the Ganges, the Meghna and the Brahmaputra. There have always been storms and floods here. None was worse than the cyclone that struck the area at midnight on November 13, 1970.

The storm was followed by a tidal wave that swept up the the river estuaries from the sea, washing away twenty-five island communities. When the waters receded, the delta had been transformed. River channels had been blocked by mud, and new ones created.

Rescue efforts were hampered by political turmoil in Bangladesh. The delay meant that thousands of corpses polluted water supplies, causing widespread disease. Crops were ruined, and people began to die from starvation. Estimates of the total loss of life varied from 300,000 to over one million.

▲ Survivors from a village in southern Bangladesh wade to safety through the water.

The 1970 cyclone marked the beginning of a terrible period in Bangladesh's history. In 1971, civil war broke out. When this ended, Bangladesh suffered a series of military coups, bringing chaos to a country that desperately needed stability.

▼ A farm in southern Bangladesh, its buildings destroyed, is completely surrounded by flood water.

Hurricane Fifi
1974

On September 18, 1974, the cyclone that weather forecasters named "Hurricane Fifi" suddenly swung toward Honduras. Torrential rain and winds of over 110 mph raged across the landscape. By the time it was all over, 11,000 Hondurans were dead and another 600,000 were homeless.

Most of the damage and loss of life was caused by flooding. In one town, Choloma, a dam gave way under the weight of water and debris, and about half of the town's population of 6,000 were drowned. Another town, Cruz Laguna, along with its 1,500 inhabitants, disappeared completely underwater.

Three-quarters of the banana plantations—the basis of the Honduran economy—were destroyed. Over 7,000 sq. miles of land were coated with a layer of mud 20 feet deep. Thousands of survivors were trapped on the roof of their houses, in trees and on dikes. Roads, railroads and harbor installations had been swept away.

The hurricane season in the Caribbean runs from June to November. The U.S. National Hurricane Center gives each storm a code name to help in tracking its progress. The first cyclone of the season is given a first name beginning with A, the second one beginning with B, and so on, through the alphabet.

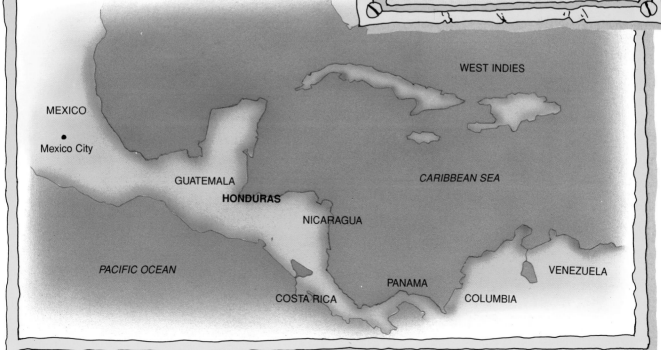

WEST INDIES

MEXICO

Mexico City

GUATEMALA

HONDURAS

NICARAGUA

CARIBBEAN SEA

PACIFIC OCEAN

COSTA RICA

PANAMA

COLUMBIA

VENEZUELA

The Darwin cyclone

1974

As the people of Darwin, capital of the Northern Territory of Australia, prepared for Christmas 1974, a cyclone was heading across the Arafura Sea between Australia and Indonesia. On Christmas Eve it swung southward, picking up speed. The cyclone struck Darwin shortly after midnight.

By 1 a.m. most of Darwin was without power and water. At the airport, aircraft were up-ended in winds of 130 mph. By dawn on Christmas Day, the entire city was a mess of rubble, and almost everyone was homeless. In view of the damage, it was lucky that only forty-nine people had been killed.

The destruction was so complete that it was necessary to evacuate the city to allow it to be rebuilt. Over the next few days 25,000 people were airlifted out, and another 10,000 left by road.

▼ About 90 percent of Darwin's buildings were destroyed by the cyclone. High winds and flying debris made the roads unsafe.

Satellites that monitor weather conditions all over the world twenty-four hours a day, are able to give people in danger zones warnings of storms through local radio and television. The U.S. National Hurricane Center aims to give twelve hours warning of approaching hurricanes.

Europe's October hurricane
1987

On October 15, 1987, millions of people in Britain went to bed expecting no more than the blustery night that had been forecast. They were in for a shock.

A fierce storm traveling up the coast of western Europe strengthened as it blew northward. By 1 a.m. on October 16, high winds were sweeping across northern France. As the winds increased to hurricane force, with gusts of up to 135 mph, the storm crossed the English Channel.

At 4 a.m., with the wind approaching 100 mph, the storm hit London. Roofs were blown off, roads were blocked, trains were canceled and aircraft were grounded. The hurricane left behind eighteen dead, hundreds of injuries and millions of dollars' worth of damage.

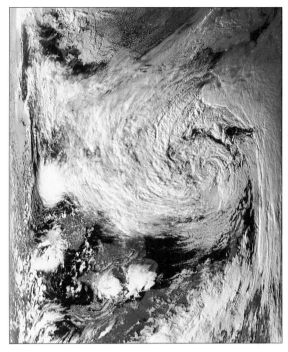

▲ This satellite picture shows the storm over Britain. The center of the spiral storm is visible on the right.

▼ Many tall trees were uprooted during the hurricane of October 1987.

Among the casualties of the hurricane was the collection of rare trees from all over the world in the Botanical Gardens at Kew in London. It will be 200 years before replacement trees will have grown sufficiently to restore the gardens to their former condition.

Bangladesh cyclone
1991

The river plains of Bangladesh were once again the locations for disaster in 1991, when a cyclone swept in from the Bay of Bengal, lashing the unprotected coastline. Over 250,000 people died in the storm and its aftermath.

On April 30, waves up to 20 feet high rolled in from the sea along the whole of the coast of Bangladesh, driven by winds that reached speeds of 145 mph. The waves were accompanied by torrential rain. Millions of acres of crops waiting to be harvested were destroyed.

Entire communities were swept away, and millions of people were marooned amid the flood waters without food, drink, shelter, or medical care, surrounded by the floating corpses of their dead livestock. Ten million people—one-tenth of Bangladesh's population—were made homeless. Because the floods had ruined the harvest, they led to famine. Many survivors fell victim to cholera, a disease caused by drinking polluted water.

▲ Thousands of square miles around Bangladesh's cyclone-prone river deltas became submerged in water in 1991.

Every year the waters of the rivers Ganges and Brahmaputra, which flow through Bangladesh, are swollen by the melting of snow in the Himalayas. This increased flow often coincides with the monsoon, a period of continuous heavy rain. In 1974, the monsoon lasted for seven weeks, with an average of nearly 5 inches of rain each day.

▼ Many people were forced to take to boats during the flooding that was caused by the cyclone.

The Sahel drought

1970 onward

The Sahel region stretches west to east across Africa, from Mauritania to Ethiopia, south of the Sahara Desert. Until the late 1960s, the land provided a reasonable living for the people who lived there. Years of drought were followed by years of above-average rainfall, which provided good crops to store for the bad years.

Since 1970, however, there have been no good years. Each year has brought a drought. Grassland has died and crops have failed. Animals have been unable to find food, and the people of the region have been on the brink of starvation. In 1985 and 1986, more than one million people in the Sahel died from starvation and disease. International relief efforts have been mounted, but are hindered by transport problems and civil wars.

Many people of the Sahel, those who are still strong enough to travel, move to the cities, causing health and housing problems there. Since 1960, the population of Mauritania's capital city, Nouakchott, has grown from less than 20,000 to nearly 400,000.

▼ The problem is too great to be solved by emergency feeding alone. The world's richer nations need to help the people of the Sahel find long-term solutions for coping with the change in climate.

The Australian drought
1990 onward

Australian farmers are used to extreme climatic conditions. When, in 1990, drought began to affect Queensland, they expected that it would soon end. They were wrong. The sky remained clear, the sun blazed down, and no rain fell.

Four years later, Queensland and the bordering state of New South Wales were still gripped by the worst drought for a hundred years. Farming was so badly affected that wheat had to be imported, for only the second time since Australia was colonized. The cotton crop in 1994 was only half that of two years before.

Millions of sheep faced slaughter because there was not enough water for them to drink. Hundreds of farming families were forced to leave their land and try to find work in the cities. But many could not even do that because the drought left them with crippling debts.

▲ Many lakes (like this salt lake) dried up, and water had to be brought in from elsewhere. Kangaroos and other creatures grazed the land dry, leaving the soil to be caught up in windstorms.

A previous serious drought in Australia occurred in 1982 and 1983. Australians named it "the Big Dry." No rain fell for two years, but when it came it was so heavy that it caused the worst flooding for a decade.

▼ In this area there is some vegetation left which will stop the soil being blown away, but the ground is still parched.

The wreck of the Spanish Armada
1588

By the end of the summer of 1588, Spain's attempt to invade England had failed. The Spanish Armada—130 ships carrying 30,000 men—had entered the English Channel from the west on July 29, 1588. Ten days later, off the French coast, an English fleet half the size delivered a crushing defeat to the Spanish. The surviving Spanish ships, many badly damaged, could not risk returning west through the Channel, so they set sail on an eastward course that would take them around the coast of Scotland and out into the Atlantic.

The damaged fleet had reached Cape Wrath, on Scotland's northwestern coast, when it met the first of a wave of fierce Atlantic storms. Leaking and crippled, crewed by starving and sick men, the ships were swept helplessly backward and forward as the wind changed.

Many were driven on to the rocks. Others were simply swamped and disappeared beneath the waves. The storms raged for a month. Further ships were lost off the coast of Ireland.

▲ This map of 1588 shows the English ships off the south coast of England chasing the Spanish fleet. The English ships were smaller and more maneuverable.

Many of the Spanish sailors were shipwrecked more than once. The crews of two ships that had been wrecked crammed onto a third ship, the *Girona*. With 1,300 men on board, its captain sailed on—only to be dashed on the rocks with the loss of all but ten men.

Thousands of men drowned. Many of the survivors who managed to scramble ashore in Ireland were killed or starved to death. Of the 130 fine Spanish ships that had set out for England, only half managed to limp home.

◀ The Spanish were not ready for the howling gales that met them as they entered the Atlantic. Many ships sank very quickly.

Cyprus locust swarm
1881

Locusts are insects that belong to the grasshopper family. They are found in many parts of the world, but are particularly common in southeastern Asia and Africa. They range in length from about 2 to 4 inches. When weather conditions are favorable for breeding, large numbers of young locusts are produced and they gather together in huge swarms. These swarms then take flight in search of new breeding grounds. When they settle, they completely destroy the vegetation.

One of the worst plagues of locusts hit the island of Cyprus, in the Mediterranean, in 1881. The swarms arrived from North Africa and settled on Cyprus to breed. Enormous damage was done to crops, and it seemed that there might be worse to come when the eggs hatched and the young started to feed. Further damage was avoided when local people got together to collect the eggs. A total of 1,280 tons of eggs were collected and destroyed.

Swarms of locusts still bring destruction to tropical and subtropical areas of the world. They can be controlled by insecticides sprayed from the air, but disputes between neighboring countries often make effective control difficult to achieve.

▼ A swarm of locusts can contain up to one billion insects, cover up to 12 sq. miles, and travel hundreds of miles. The arrival of locusts means devastation for crops in agricultural areas.

The great London smog
1952

London today is a clean city compared with how it was in 1952. In those days, there were coal-burning power stations and factories not far from the center of the city. Most homes were heated by coal fires. Steam locomotives, powered by coal, hauled many trains into the capital. And there were few controls on fumes from cars and lorries.

Carbon, sulfur and other chemical fumes from all these sources filled the air. In foggy conditions, the chemicals mixed with the fog and produced a heavily polluted blanket of "smog." This was what happened on December 5, 1952, when a massive cloud of fog descended on London. It hung over the city for five days, steadily getting more dirty and more poisonous. The weight of smoke in the air of central London increased by almost ten times.

The smog affected thousands of sufferers from bronchitis, asthma and other diseases affecting the lungs. When at last, on December 10, the smog lifted, it was estimated that it had killed about 4,000 people, most of them elderly.

▲ Transport in London was almost paralyzed. A double-decker bus, pictured here on the fourth day of smog, moves slowly through the city with only fog lights to help it.

The main cause of smog today is pollution from vehicle exhausts. It hangs in the air all the time in large cities like Los Angeles and Mexico City. Lead-free gas and catalytic converters fitted to vehicle exhausts have helped to reduce the risk to health from this form of pollution, but it remains a serious problem.

◀ London policemen used flaming torches so that they could see and be seen in the smog of 1952.

Lake Nios
1986

The people of the villages around Lake Nios in Cameroon, in western central Africa, thought they heard thunder as they settled down for the night on August 21, 1986. But what they had heard was something far more serious. By morning, 1,700 people would be dead.

Lake Nios lies in the crater of an extinct volcano. Beneath it, deep below the surface of the Earth's crust, lies molten rock. The "thunder" that the villagers heard was an underground volcanic explosion that sent a cloud of poisonous carbon dioxide gas bubbling up to the lake's surface. Perhaps because of changes in atmospheric pressure, instead of rising harmlessly into the air, the colorless and odorless gas spread close to the ground through the lakeside villages. Families and livestock were suffocated as they slept. In one village, only two out of 700 people survived.

The Lake Nios disaster was not discovered until two days later, when a government official checked out a traveler's story. He found the area peaceful, but deadly quiet. Then, to his horror, he realized that every person and every animal—including even the insects—was dead.

Extinct volcanoes that continue to emit gases exist in other parts of the world. One example is the Solfatara near Naples in Italy. The volcano last erupted about 900 years ago, but steam and poisonous fumes continue to rise from it.

▲ Today Lake Nios looks peaceful once more, nestling in its volcanic crater in Cameroon, Africa.

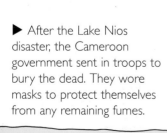

▶ After the Lake Nios disaster, the Cameroon government sent in troops to bury the dead. They wore masks to protect themselves from any remaining fumes.

The Great Fire of London

1666

At about 1 a.m. on Sunday, September 2, 1666, fire broke out in a baker's shop in Pudding Lane in the City of London. A fresh wind blew the flames quickly through the narrow streets of timber houses and into the warehouses on the north bank of the Thames River.

The fire swept through the city, destroying everything in its path. Londoners fled in their hundreds of thousands to safety in the hills north of the city. Soldiers were called in to pull down houses to make a gap that the flames could not cross, but this tactic failed. On the fourth night, the wind dropped and the flames died down.

The damage was terrible. The old St Paul's Cathedral, eighty-seven parish churches, many of the city's important commercial buildings, countless shops, and over 13,000 houses had been destroyed. Fortunately, few lives had been lost.

▲ The damage caused by the fire was so great it took fifty years to rebuild the city.

A new St Paul's Cathedral, designed by Sir Christopher Wren, was completed in 1712. Its magnificent dome became one of London's most famous landmarks. The cathedral narrowly escaped destruction in air raids on London in World War II, and it can still be seen, nestling amid the modern buildings of the City of London.

▼ This map shows the area affected by the fire. Only one-fifth of the old city remained standing.

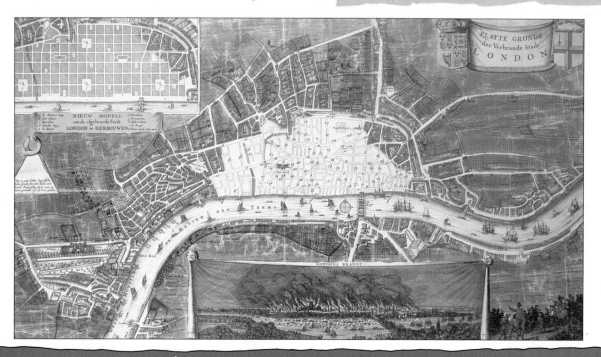

The Chicago fire
1871

Between 1831 and 1871, Chicago, Illinois, grew into a major city, and timber homes were hastily built to house the settlers who moved there.

The summer of 1871 was dry. When fire broke out on the west side of the city on October 8, it was carried by the wind through the timber buildings, leaping the river and setting fire to both the north and south sides of the city.

In the south, gunpowder was used to destroy buildings in the path of the flames and create a successful firebreak. However, the fire raged on the north side until it was put out by rain twenty-seven hours later. By that time, 250 people had been killed and 100,000 made homeless. Over 17,000 buildings were destroyed.

▼ Chicago was devastated by the fire, with wooden buildings very badly affected. It took about three years to rebuild the flattened city.

To escape the flames, thousands of Chicago people fled in panic to the shore of Lake Michigan. Some, fearing that the fire would not stop until it reached the water, leaped into the lake and were drowned.

The São Paulo fire
1965

São Paulo is Brazil's largest city, and its main commercial center. In the 1960s, it had grown rapidly, and the need to find space for office workers outstripped the concern for safety. In 1965, a fire broke out in a skyscraper that had been designed with no fire protection. It started on one of the lower floors of the building. Before anyone had noticed it, it had taken hold. The staircases and elevator shafts acted as chimneys, carrying the flames rapidly upward. Within two minutes, the bottom ten floors of the building were on fire.

People working on the upper floors were trapped. They fled in panic to the roof, hoping to be rescued by the fire department or by helicopter. But the fire had spread too rapidly, and within only 20 minutes, 227 people were dead.

▼ Fire can spread with frightening speed, especially through dry wooded areas.

The São Paulo fire was caused by a "flashover." What was at first a minor fire became unstoppable when hot gases exploded into flames as a result of contact with a fresh supply of oxygen – probably let in by someone opening a door. From that moment on, the people in the skyscraper were doomed.

Australian bush fire

1983

In 1982 and 1983, Australia suffered a severe drought that dried up thousands of square miles of grassland and forest. In February 1983, something—perhaps a discarded cigarette butt—set an area of eucalyptus trees on fire near the city of Melbourne. Soon, the whole forest was a sea of flames. Steadily, the flames began to close in on three sides of Melbourne. The small timber-built town of Macedon, outside Melbourne, was reduced to charred rubble. By the time it stopped, the fire had killed seventy-five people. Over 1,275 sq. miles of trees and crops were destroyed.

Bush fires are a constant threat in many parts of Australia. Their severity is increased by summer winds that blow when the vegetation is dry and fan the flames. Ever aware of this risk, whole communities volunteer to help in case of fire, and provide support for the professional fire-fighting crews.

▲ Eucalyptus trees contain oil that acts as a fuel, helping to keep the fire burning.

▼ In 1982, the ground in the Australian bush was so dry, just a spark was enough to set it ablaze.

Chinese forest fire

1987

It was a windy day in the early summer of 1987 when a forester in northeastern China set off to clear an area of undergrowth with a mechanical cutter. Unknown to him, the machine was leaking oil. This caught fire—perhaps from a carelessly dropped cigarette butt—and triggered off a major disaster.

Fanned by the strong winds, the fire was soon out of control. Within a day, a wall of flames 112 miles long was advancing through the forest. Five towns were razed to the ground, killing 200 people, and destroying 2,320 sq. miles of forest.

Expert firefighters were sent from all over China, backed up by a force of 50,000 troops. A firebreak 75 miles wide was hacked through the forest. Meanwhile, aircraft sprayed rain-making chemicals above the flames. The fire was eventually put out, but not before it had destroyed a large part of China's timber reserves and rendered the land unusable for years.

▲ Fire warnings such as this are common in wooded areas all over the world. During dry weather, the smallest spark can start a fire.

The smallest spark, or even the Sun's rays shining through a broken bottle, can start a devastating forest fire if strong winds are blowing. This risk is greatest in fall, when the ground is covered with dry, dead leaves, needles and cones.

Constantinople plague

AD 542

In April AD 542, the citizens of Constantinople, the capital of the Byzantine Empire, were worried. Many of them were becoming ill with a sudden fever, followed by swellings and pain so excruciating that they were driven mad. The victims suffered from delusions, some believing that those looking after them were in fact intending to kill them.

The disease that had struck them was bubonic plague, which had been moving through the eastern Mediterranean. It spread quickly in the crowded streets of Constantinople. People who looked after plague victims became exhausted.

The plague ravaged the city for four months. At its height, the plague killed 10,000 people a day. There were too few people well enough to bury the dead, and the unburied bodies added to the spread of disease.

By August, the number of plague cases had begun to fall, although the disease continued to claim victims throughout the following winter. Many who recovered were left with speech defects or partial paralysis for the rest of their lives.

> The first appearance of bubonic plague in the western world was in the first century AD, when there was an outbreak in Libya, Egypt and Syria. From there, it spread through the Roman Empire. Outbreaks of the disease tormented Europe for the next fifteen centuries.

▼ The emperor Justinian, shown in this mosaic, caught the plague but made a remarkable recovery. His illness was kept a secret from his people.

The Black Death
1348–1390

In 1348, an epidemic of the disease known as the plague began to spread across Europe. It had spread along caravan trade routes from China to the Middle East, and had then been carried to Europe by ship. Among the symptoms of one form of the disease was the appearance of dark blotches on the victim's skin. This is why this particular outbreak of plague became known as the "Black Death." For those who caught the disease, a painful death was almost inevitable. There was no cure.

The germs that cause the plague were carried by fleas, which lived in the fur of the black rat. In the fourteenth century, the black rat population was enormous, and once the disease had arrived it spread rapidly. Between 1348 and 1350, 25 million Europeans died of the

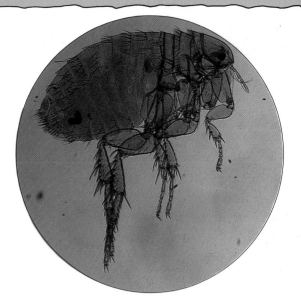

▲ The Indian rat flea, carrier of the deadly plague or "Black Death."

The Black Death killed an estimated one-third of the human population of Europe, but it was good news for cats. They had often been associated with witchcraft and evil, but their ability to catch black rats now made them popular. Once the Black Death had passed, however, so did the cats' popularity.

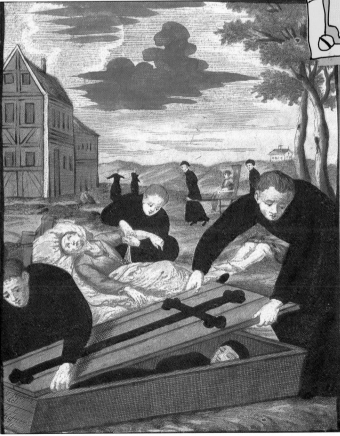

Black Death, but this was not the end of the epidemic. It recurred again and again over the next forty years.

So many people died during the Black Death that there was a great shortage of workers. Whole villages were abandoned. Farms went untended and as a result food production fell. The Black Death was followed by starvation in many parts of Europe.

◀ There were serious outbreaks of plague all through the sixteenth and seventeenth centuries. These Jesuit priests are taking plague victims out of the town to nurse them. Those who died were quickly buried.

Smallpox in the Americas
1519–1540

When Spanish troops invaded Mexico in 1519, they took with them, without knowing it, the deadly disease smallpox. Highly contagious, smallpox began with severe aches and pains, followed by high fever and a disfiguring rash. It was usually fatal. The few survivors were left scarred and sometimes blind.

Smallpox was at that time unknown in Mexico, and the native people had not had the chance to build up resistance to it. It swept through the country over the next three years, killing between two and three million native Mexicans. The Spanish also introduced the disease to South America when they attacked the Inca Empire.

Smallpox may be the answer to the riddle of the lost Inca city of Machu Picchu, which was discovered, almost perfectly preserved, in 1911. The city was abandoned, with no sign of fighting, at about the time of the Spanish invasion. Some archaeologists think that the inhabitants of the city died of smallpox.

▲ A nineteenth-century doctor vaccinates a patient against smallpox. The patient was infected with cowpox, a milder but similar disease, and would then be protected from the deadly smallpox.

Ergot poisoning
1816

In 1816, in the Lorraine and Burgundy regions of eastern France, large numbers of people began to experience strange symptoms, including numbness in their hands and feet, and itching. Nervous fits followed. These became more serious and frequent until the victims died. Doctors were unable to find a cure. Although whole families went down with the symptoms, the illness did not appear to be infectious—that is, it did not spread from one person to another.

What had attacked the people of Lorraine and Burgundy was a form of food poisoning. Their diet was made up mainly of black rye bread. Part of the rye crop had been infected with ergot, a type of fungus. The fungus can grow on rye and contains a poison that attacks the nervous system if eaten.

Rye bread is a basic food in northern Europe and there have been many outbreaks of ergot poisoning since the Middle Ages. However, the French outbreak was the worst for many centuries. Fortunately, diseased rye can be easily detected, and it was probably only the chaos following the end of the Napoleonic Wars that allowed the diseased grain to escape notice in 1816.

One of the worst outbreaks of food poisoning in the twentieth century was in Morocco in 1959. Mineral oil that contained a dangerous chemical was sold as cooking oil. Over 10,000 Moroccans suffered almost instant paralysis when they ate food cooked in the oil.

▼ A healthy field of rye grows free of the ergot fungus, which is usually easy to detect.

Cholera outbreak
1817–1832

Cholera is a disease that is caused by bacteria in water contaminated by sewage. Throughout history, it has been common in India and southeast Asia, but in 1817, a particularly violent and deadly form of cholera broke out in Calcutta, India. Over the next fifteen years it spread westward to infect most of the rest of the world. Like the Black Death earlier (see page 59), it was carried by travelers, traders and sailors.

People in Europe began to panic as reports of the epidemic started to arrive from northern India, Afghanistan and Persia. By 1830, cholera had reached Russia, and some European countries tried to restrict incoming travelers. In the English Channel, British warships intercepted cargo ships from infected places. But the disease marched on.

By 1831, it had reached Britain, where it caused 78,000 deaths. Ships then carried cholera across the Atlantic to North America.

Cholera struck fast and without warning. In those days, there was no known cure and it was almost always fatal. One in twenty Russians died in the 1830 outbreak, and one in thirty Poles. By 1832, the epidemic had died down. It broke out again many more times during the nineteenth century—but never again with such devastating effect.

A British doctor, John Snow, proved that cholera was passed on in infected drinking water. He traced the source of an 1854 outbreak in London to a single street pump that had been contaminated by sewage. His work showed the importance of giving homes a supply of pure water for drinking and cooking.

▲ This caricature of 1832 shows how some doctors, unfamiliar with cholera, used strange treatment methods in their attempts to combat the disease.

▼ In Cairo, Egypt, and many other places where cholera was rife, people burned sulfur and tar in the streets to act as a disinfectant.

The Irish Famine

1845–1849

Ireland in the 1840s was as poor as any country in Europe. Five out of six Irish families lived in one-room huts, often made of mud. They ate mainly potatoes, the crop that grew best in the exhausted soil of their small plots of land.

In the wet summer of 1845, the Irish potato crop was struck by blight, a disease that made the potatoes rotten, making them inedible. Blight-infected seed was used again the next year, and the blight got worse. In 1848 and 1849, blight struck again. The Irish were desperate. They were starving to death and had no resistance to disease. They were unable to pay the rent on their land, and landlords turned them out of their homes, often setting the huts on fire so that they could not be reoccupied.

Ireland was part of the United Kingdom, but the British government did little. About one million Irish people died of either hunger or disease. Another million left for England, North America or Australasia. These two million made up one-quarter of Ireland's 1845 population.

Many Americans, Canadians, Australians and New Zealanders can trace their families back to the Irish emigrants of the 1840s. But Irish emigration continued throughout the second half of the nineteenth century. Between 1845 and 1925, it was estimated that nearly five million Irish people had emigrated to the United States.

Phylloxera infestation

1860s

France is the world's leading wine-producing nation. In the 1860s, a plant disease that affects grapevines brought disaster to French wine producers.

Between 1858 and 1863, vines were brought in from the United States to improve the quality of the grape crop. Unknown to anyone, the imported vines were infested by insects—the grape phylloxera. This feeds on the sap of the vine and stunts its growth. Female phylloxera lay their eggs on the stems of the vine, and these in turn produce more insects, which attack the host plant before flying off the next year to infect other vines. Leaves and grapes fail to form properly, and eventually the roots of the vine wither and rot.

Phylloxera was first discovered in France in 1863, but by that time the infestation was already out of control. Over the next few years about 2.5 million acres of vineyards were destroyed. The only answer proved to be to dig up all the infected vines and replace them with new plants that were resistant to phylloxera. But it takes time to establish a vineyard, and it was many years before the French wine industry recovered. Most French wine is now produced from vines grafted onto phylloxera-resistant American roots.

Chile is one of the few wine-growing regions unaffected by phylloxera. Its wine-growing industry was established with vines imported from France in 1851 – before the arrival of the disease there. Its isolated situation has since protected it from the spread of the disease. With the destruction of the French vineyards, the Chilean vines are now the only survivors of the original French vines.

▲ France has reestablished itself as a major wine producer—thanks largely to the American rootstocks on to which European vines are grafted.

▼ The adult grape phylloxera under the microscope. It lives in the roots of the grapevine and lays its eggs on the stems.

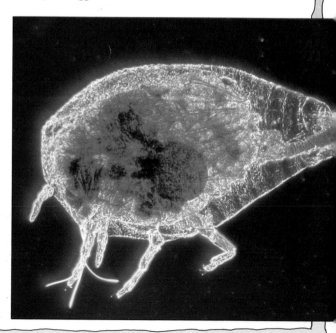

Chinese drought and famine

1870s

One of the worst human disasters in history struck China in the 1870s. The monsoon—the period of continuous rain on which China relies for most of its water supplies—failed in 1876 and the two following years. There were no reserves of grain, and famine soon set in.

People were forced to eat whatever they could find. The small amount of grain on the market fetched huge prices, and some families had to sell their houses and furniture to stay alive.

Thousands sailed across the Gulf of Chihli (now Bo Hai) to Manchuria, in northeastern China, when they were told that grain was cheaper there, but the increased demand soon raised prices. Travelers reported seeing villages with piles of starved corpses at the gate. Three-quarters of the population had died either of starvation or of diseases caused in the poor conditions of the famine. All together between 9 and 13 million Chinese people are believed to have lost their lives.

▲ During the famine people tried any source of food. Some tried the bark of trees. There were even reports of cannibalism in some areas.

Desperate people will go to any lengths to find food for themselves and their families. In the 1870s, the Chinese government imposed a cruel punishment on people caught stealing food. They were nailed up in wooden cages, called "sorrow cages," and left to starve.

◄ Even those who survived the famine suffered terribly. Diseases such as cholera and bubonic plague were rife.

Influenza
1918–1919

Today, we do not think of influenza (or flu) as a fatal disease except when it strikes the elderly or people who are already sick. Yet the flu epidemic that began in 1918 killed 21 million people across the world.

The outbreak began in Europe in May 1918 among soldiers fighting in World War I. The disease spread quickly through the crowded trenches and camps. By July, it had also infected large numbers of civilians in mainland Europe, but most people suffered only mildly.

Influenza returned in the autumn, this time in a stronger, more deadly form, and the death toll began to increase as the bacteria were carried all over the world. Young people were badly hit, possibly because older people had built up resistance during earlier outbreaks. By the time the epidemic had died down in 1919, it had killed twice as many people as had been killed in World War I.

▲ A street cleaner in New York wears a mask as protection from germs that cause influenza and are passed on by coughs and sneezes.

▼ The outbreak spread from Europe to Japan. Here children wore cloth masks as protection from flu.

Influenza epidemics continue to sweep across the world every few years, but advances in medicine have reduced their dangers. Vaccines are available that prevent some types of influenza, while sufferers are treated with antibiotics that reduce the severity of the disease.

AIDS
1980s onward

Early in the 1980s, doctors began to notice that some people seemed to have lost their ability to resist certain infections, including rare forms of pneumonia and cancer. They gave this loss of resistance the name AIDS (Acquired Immune Deficiency Syndrome). In 1983, researchers found that people with AIDS had been infected by a virus which they called HIV (Human Immunodeficiency Virus).

We do not know whether everyone who has the HIV virus will develop AIDS, but some doctors believe that about one-third of infected people will do so. The virus enters the bloodstream through breaks in the skin. The use of infected needles by drug-takers, sex with infected people, and the use of infected blood during blood transfusions are all ways in which HIV can be passed on.

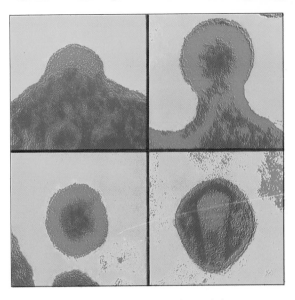

▲ The HIV virus. It has been estimated that over 600,000 people have developed AIDS, but the number who have the HIV virus, and are therefore at risk, is unknown.

When the HIV virus was first identified, some doctors predicted that it would spread rapidly throughout the world's population and become the greatest plague of the twentieth century. This has not happened, partly because of the success of efforts to educate people about ways of avoiding the disease.

▼ A giant quilt made by people in the U.S. commemorates the victims of AIDS. It contains the names of hundreds of people who have died as a result of AIDS.

Deforestation in Europe

c. 1500

For thousands of years, most of Britain and northwestern Europe was covered in dense forests of broad-leaved trees. From about two thousand years ago, the forests began to shrink as they were cleared and taken over for farming. Wood was the main fuel for heating in the home and for industry. It was also in demand for building houses and ships.

By the sixteenth century, trees were being felled at such a rate that the situation in Europe reached crisis point. A shortage of wood for charcoal threatened the iron and glass-making industries, which used huge quantities in their furnaces. Wood for fuel in homes jumped in price. The trees could not be replaced fast enough. The great European forests had gone forever.

The shrinking of the forests interfered with the natural drainage of the land and created marshes in many places. These areas have now been replanted with trees to restore them.

▲ Today, less than one-tenth of the forests that once existed are still standing. The rest have gone forever, like this one in northwestern Scotland.

Deforestation changed European history. Homes and industry increasingly turned to coal as a fuel. Over the next 300 years, the use of coal led to the invention of the steam engine and the concentration of work in factories.

Rabbits in Australia

1859

Rabbits are not native to Australia and until 1859 there were none there. But in that year a farmer introduced a colony of twenty-four wild rabbits from England. Little did he know that he was about to cause an agricultural disaster.

In Australia, rabbits had few natural enemies, and within a few decades they had become a major problem. They ate crops, destroyed newly planted seeds, nibbled the bark and buds of young trees and damaged fields and banks by burrowing. Fencing could not keep them out of the farmers' fields.

In 1950, a new method of controlling the rabbits was tried. Myxomatosis, a disease that kills rabbits, was introduced into Australia. Mosquitoes were infected with the disease and the insects infected the rabbits. Once introduced, myxomatosis passed quickly through the whole rabbit population. In southeastern Australia, almost 80 percent of the rabbit population was wiped out.

▲ Rabbits became a problem in such a short time because they breed very quickly. One female can produce up to twenty-five young each year.

Myxomatosis was introduced to Europe in 1952 when a French landowner released two infected rabbits. Within a few months it had spread across Europe and even across the sea to Britain. By the end of 1953, only two out of every thousand of Europe's rabbits were still alive.

The Halifax explosion
1917

The harbor of Halifax, Nova Scotia, Canada, has been the scene of great dramas. Into this harbor steamed the rescue ships from the *Titanic,* which sank when it hit an iceberg in 1912. Some of the 1,513 victims of that tragedy are buried in the cemetery at the harborside. It was in this harbor too that a massive explosion took place on December 7, 1917, when a French freighter called *Mont Blanc,* packed with 5,000 tons of explosives, collided with another ship, the *Imo.*

One observer wrote at the time that in a brief moment, "nearly 2,000 people were hurled into eternity, 6,000 were maimed and blinded, 10,000 rendered homeless, and $35,000,000 worth of property was destroyed." The death count was later fixed at 1,635, which made this the world's worst accidental explosion.

Luckily, the accident happened in a part of the harbor called the Narrows, where a hill turned away the full force of the explosion from reaching the center of Halifax town, but the entire hillside was swept bare. The explosion was felt and the blast of air broke windows as far away as Truro, over 60 miles away. A ship's anchor was whisked off through the air. A column of smoke rose as from a volcano, so high that it could be seen by half the island of Nova Scotia.

> The explosion set off one of the greatest snowstorms that Halifax had ever known. During that night nearly 2 feet of snow fell, in some places smothering people who were already dying, in others covering up the bodies of the dead.

▼ The scene of total devastation after the horrific blast at Halifax harbor.

San Joaquin Valley subsidence
1920s–1960s

The San Joaquin Valley runs southeast to northwest between Bakersfield and Oakland in California. It is an area that sees only a small amount of rain. Despite this, the valley is intensively farmed. Water for irrigation is pumped from beneath the valley floor. The use of irrigation in the area began as early as 1780, but the volume of water used increased hugely from the beginning of the twentieth century. By 1920, over 2 million acres of land in the valley were being irrigated—almost three times as much as in 1900.

The result was inevitable. Large areas of the valley began to subside—in some places by up to 30 feet. The land movement destroyed wells and irrigation channels, and brought ruin to many farmers. Unless pumping was stopped, farming in the San Joaquin valley would be destroyed.

It was not until the 1960s that the Californian government finally faced up to the danger. The pumping of water from beneath the valley was stopped, and water was brought instead from the Sierra Nevada mountains. Land in the San Joaquin Valley is still subsiding, but at a far slower rate. Scientists hope that, in time, the land will stabilize again.

> Any human activity underground, such as coal mining, can cause subsidence, but subsidence also occurs naturally. Some parts of the Fens in eastern England have fallen by as much as 13 feet over the past century because their peat soil has dried out.

▼ A vast area of land in the San Joaquin Valley, California, has subsided during the twentieth century.

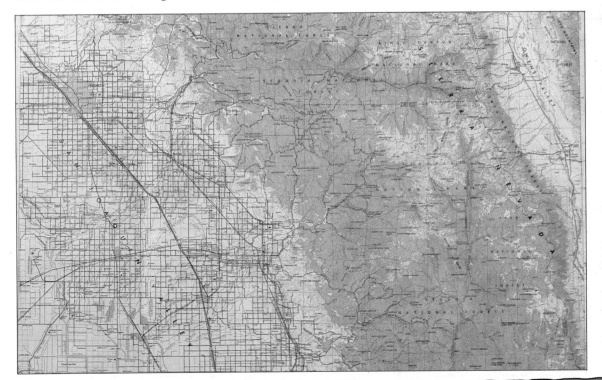

The American Dust Bowl

1930s

The first settlers in the Midwest used their land for grazing cattle. However, the invention of the tractor in the early twentieth century meant that the farmers were able to plow land to grow wheat.

But disaster struck in the early 1930s. There was a drought and the wheat crop failed. The plowed soil was left bare and dry, and without grass to hold it together, the fierce westerly winds caused dust storms. The devastated area of farmland was called the Dust Bowl. It covered 25,000 sq. miles.

The size of the problem jolted the state and federal governments into action. The Dust Bowl area was gradually brought back to life by bringing water to the parched land, restoring the grassland and by encouraging more responsible and forward-looking farming methods.

▲ Dust storms up to 5 miles high were common in Oklahoma, and also in neighboring Kansas and Texas. Many farmers from this area had to move west to California to find work.

The story of the Dust Bowl inspired the American author John Steinbeck to write his best-selling novel *The Grapes of Wrath*. It describes the plight of a Dust Bowl farming family forced to leave their land. It was later made into a film.

▼ Tens of thousands of farmers in the Midwest were ruined by the Dust Bowl.

DDT
1950s

In 1939, there was what seemed to be good news for the world's farmers and for areas where tropical diseases such as malaria flourished. A new, "safe" insecticide called DDT (short for dichlorodiphenyltrichloroethane) had been invented. It killed insects on contact by paralyzing their nervous systems. It could be sprayed on crops or over the areas, such as swamps, where disease-carrying insects bred.

Over the next thirty years, millions of tons of DDT were used throughout the world. It may have saved millions of lives in Africa. By eliminating damaging insect pests, farmers achieved huge increases in their crops. But before long, scientists began to worry. Some insects developed resistance to DDT, making it less effective than before. Also, it was discovered that DDT was accumulating in the bodies of plant-eating animals that ate DDT-sprayed plants. DDT was not broken down inside the animals and there was concern that it would then pass into the food chain.

▲ A farmworker sprays insecticide on his crops in Papua New Guinea. Modern insecticides are more easily broken down by animals than DDT.

The first warning signs of DDT buildup came from a study of birds. The DDT they had absorbed from insects they had eaten caused them to lay eggs with thin shells. These broke too soon, leaving the young to die. If DDT could affect birds, what might it be doing to humans?

◀ Scientists and ecologists came to the conclusion that DDT was doing more harm than good and its use was restricted in the United States in 1972. It is now completely banned in the United States, Europe and many other countries.

Thalidomide
1950s and 1960s

In the 1950s, scientists came up with a new drug that was said to control stress during pregnancy, preventing nausea and helping women to sleep soundly. It was called thalidomide. Developed in the United States and first prescribed in 1957, it later became available in Europe.

By 1960, doctors began to be alarmed at the number of babies being born with shortened limbs, and sometimes other abnormalities. The cause was found to be thalidomide. In 1961, the drug was banned, but by this time about 8,000 babies around the world had been affected.

After a long legal battle, the drug company that developed thalidomide agreed to compensate the victims. Thalidomide had been sold without careful testing for possible side-effects. The story of the "thalidomide children" remains a terrible reminder of the need for any new drug to be thoroughly tested before being prescribed, particularly to pregnant women.

▲ An American victim of thalidomide has learned to paint with her only hand.

Not every mother who took thalidomide gave birth to a handicapped baby, but the chances of doing so were so high, and the results so devastating, that the drug was withdrawn from sale as soon as its dangers became known. Nowadays, drug companies are much more careful about testing new drugs.

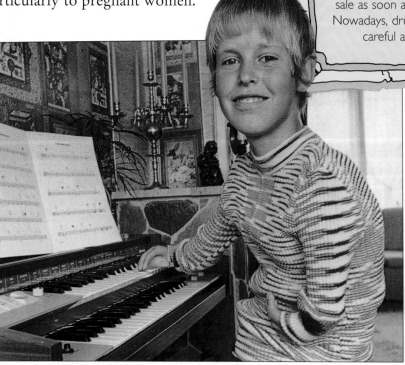

◀ Martin Snijders was Holland's first "thalidomide child." Even when quite young, he learned to live with his disability, developing a range of skills including playing the electric organ.

Kyshtym
1958

What may possibly have been one of the world's greatest disasters is shrouded in mystery. It happened at Kyshtym, a town about 60 miles from the industrial city of Chelyabinsk in Siberia. It was in 1958, when relations were hostile between the communist countries, led by the then USSR, and the capitalist countries allied to the United States.

The Soviet government of that time never released details of major disasters. It kept especially quiet about this one because it involved nuclear material that may have been used in the development of secret nuclear weapons. All that is known is that there was a major explosion near Kyshtym, and that the names and locations of a number of villages in the area were later removed from official Soviet maps.

Today, the explosion would have been observed by satellite, but none existed in 1958. Was there an explosion of nuclear waste? Did a nuclear weapon go off by accident? What happened at Kyshtym? As yet, no one outside Russia knows.

▲ One of the weapons developed in the Soviet Union was the SS1, which could carry a nuclear warhead or an ordinary high-explosive one.

In 1958, the Soviet Union was trying desperately to catch up with the United States in the production of advanced nuclear weapons. The first Russian hydrogen bomb had been tested in 1957—five years behind the United States. It is possible that the Kyshtym explosion was connected with the production or testing of a hydrogen bomb that failed.

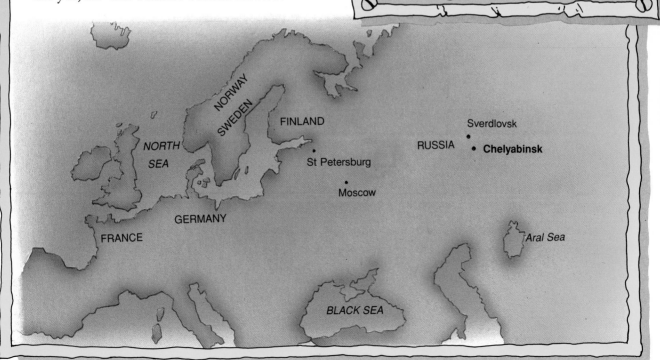

Minimata Bay pollution
1953

The cats of Minimata gave the first sign that anything was wrong in the fishing village on Kyushu, Japan's southernmost island. In 1953, they began to behave strangely, running around crazily and even drowning themselves.

Soon, people in the village started to show symptoms of disease or poisoning such as convulsions, speech difficulties and blindness. At least 150 people died or suffered permanent damage. A number of babies were born with deformities or brain damage.

A few years earlier, a factory manufacturing plastics had been built on Minimata Bay. Its wastes were discharged into the sea. Mercury in the factory wastes was poisoning the fish and the people (and cats) who ate them. But the factory owners refused to allow an inspection. It was not until ten years later that they admitted responsibility.

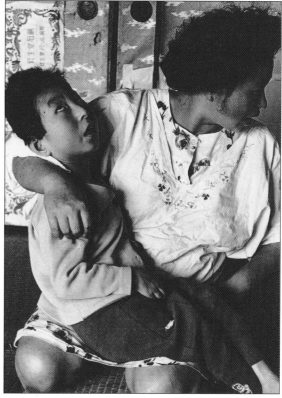

▲ A victim of the Minimata Bay disaster is cared for by her mother. Many of the victims are still alive today, some thirty years after the plastics factory closed and the tide of deadly waste stopped.

SEA OF JAPAN

NORTH KOREA

Tokyo

JAPAN

SOUTH KOREA

Osaka

Kyushu

Minimata Bay

PACIFIC OCEAN

Once taken into the body, mercury cannot be eliminated, making it a particularly deadly poison. In 1972, over ninety countries signed an international ban on the dumping of mercury in the ocean, where it can contaminate fish stocks.

The plant closed down in 1966, but by that time Minimata had been left with a grim legacy. Survivors faced lives of extreme difficulty and discomfort, followed by early and painful deaths. Many families had to care for helpless victims, many of them children. The young women of Minimata were afraid to have children in case they were mentally retarded or deformed.

Vaiont Dam collapse
1963

In September 1963, shepherds tending their flocks on the slopes of Mount Toc in the Italian Alps noticed that the sheep seemed restless. It was one of many examples of animals being aware before humans of an impending disaster. The shepherds did not have long to wait before they found out what was wrong. Below Mount Toc was the Vaiont Dam, part of a hydroelectric scheme. Behind the dam stretched a lake four miles long.

For weeks, rain had lashed at Mount Toc. Suddenly, during the night of October 9, part of the sodden mountain collapsed. Millions of tons of rock slid from the mountainside into the lake. At once, water overflowed the dam in a giant wave and swept down onto the villages below. In a few minutes, it was all over. One village, Langarone, was completely wiped out with almost everyone who lived there. Several other villages were devastated.

The Vaiont disaster showed the foolishness of not listening to expert opinion. Many geologists and engineers had advised against building a dam on the site because Mount Toc was an unstable mountain. Sadly, the experts were proved right.

▲ Few buildings stand in the shattered town of Langarone. It was impossible to search for survivors in the sea of mud after the mountain collapsed.

◀ Debris also made it hard to find survivors. No one knows how many died. The death toll certainly reached 1,800; it may have been as many as 2,500.

Yungay avalanche
1970

On May 31, 1970, a huge earthquake shook the ground along a 250-mile stretch of the coast of Peru, destroying most of a fishing town called Chimbote and killing 2,700 people. Inland in the area of Callejón de Huaylas, popular with tourists, is the mountain of Huascarán. The earthquake set off an avalanche of mud and snow that swept down its eroded slopes and swallowed up two small towns. At Yungay only the tips of the 100-foot palm trees in the town square could be seen; nearby Ranrahirca had almost disappeared.

Aircraft overflying the stricken area could do little because of the mist and dust that filled the air. Not until an amateur radio operator made a call for help, "Don't forget us!" did the outside world realize how much damage had been done. For 60 hours no helicopter could get through. Then 100 men were parachuted in, but it was many days before relief workers could reach the remoter areas. Meanwhile, hundreds of thousands of peasants were without shelter or food for almost a week.

Rescuers eventually found that the avalanche had killed about 18,000 people. A vast mass of ice and rock, 1,640 feet wide and 2 miles long, had fallen 10,000 feet almost vertically from the west face of Huascarán. The mass of ice then poured down the valley at 250 mph. Rock and earth falls dammed a river and destroyed many houses. Above Yungay, a hill 600 feet high was swept up by the avalanche and dumped on the other side of the valley.

The mountain people of Peru have great courage and spirit. On June 2, 1970, only a few days after the avalanche, Peru beat Bulgaria in a World Cup soccer match. People cheered and even planted Peruvian flags in the heaps of rubble that had been their homes.

▼ This overturned bus lies in the main square of Yungay, a city of 20,000 people before the disaster.

The Koyna Reservoir tremors
1967

Most earthquakes are the result of natural movements in the plates that make up the Earth's crust, and are unavoidable natural disasters. Sometimes, however, an earthquake can be the result of human interference with the stresses that exist in the crust, and this is what happened at Koyna, in India, in 1967.

The huge Koyna Reservoir was built in the early 1960s to provide a reliable water supply for Bombay and the surrounding district. Filling of the reservoir started in 1962. A year later, earth tremors began in what had previously been an earthquake-free region. The tremors became bigger and more frequent until, on December 10, 1967, there was a powerful earthquake that left 177 people dead and 2,300 injured, as well as causing extensive damage.

Unknown to anyone, the weight of water in the Koyna Reservoir had set up stresses in the layers of rock beneath. The earlier minor tremors were a sign of these stresses. Once the stresses had been set up, it was inevitable that one day they would be released in a major earthquake.

All earthquakes occur as a result of stresses in the fabric of the Earth's crust. Although these stresses can be measured, it is still almost impossible to predict when an earthquake will happen, exactly where it will be centered, or how big it will be.

▼ It was hoped that the Koyna Reservoir would store enough water to supply the City of Bombay. However, no one predicted that its presence would cause Earth tremors.

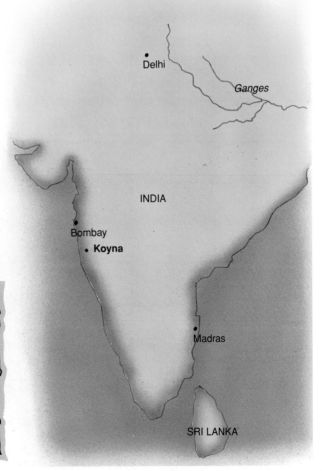

The first evidence that reservoirs could cause earthquakes emerged in the United States in the 1930s, when the giant Hoover Dam, with the Lake Mead reservoir behind it, was constructed. Between 1936 and 1939, local people experienced hundreds of minor earthquakes in an area that had previously been free of tremors.

Seveso gas leak
1976

On July 15, 1976, there was an accident at a chemical plant in Seveso, near Milan in Italy. The factory made a weedkiller, TCDD, from chemicals, including a deadly poison, dioxin. The accident released a cloud of dioxin into the atmosphere. The alarm was raised in Seveso when domestic animals began to die for no apparent reason. A mass evacuation from the village was ordered.

Humans exposed to even tiny doses of dioxin suffer an immediate blistering skin rash, but the long-term effects are far more serious. Dioxin poisoning can lead to cancer and other illnesses. It can also cause deformities in babies whose mothers have been exposed to it. What is worse, it can take many years to eliminate dioxin from the body, and it can cause medical problems long after exposure. Two weeks after the Seveso leak, one out of every six inhabitants tested was found to have symptoms of dioxin poisoning.

▲ The factory near Milan, Italy, at which the Seveso gas leak started in July 1976.

As a result of the Seveso gas leak, people and governments became more aware of the dangers of industrial accidents involving chemicals. The case for stricter safety controls on factories that use dangerous chemicals was strengthened.

◄ The first victims of the disaster were small animals such as rabbits. But the full cost of the leak in terms of human health may never be known.

The *Amoco Cadiz* oil spill

1978

In stormy weather in March 1978, the oil tanker *Amoco Cadiz* was making its way up the English Channel. Disaster struck on March 24, off the coast of Brittany. The ship's steering failed in the heavy seas. A tug arrived to take the tanker in tow, but the towline broke. The *Amoco Cadiz* drifted onto rocks and, after severe pounding by the waves, broke in two. Over 78 million gallons of oil gushed from the wreckage into the sea. Carried by the tide, it covered the beaches with a foul-smelling black slime. Thousands of seabirds died. Along the shore, shoals of dead fish were washed up. It was months before the English Channel could be declared clean again.

▲ As the ship went down, various attempts were made to clean up. Boats sprayed chemicals on the water to disperse the oil.

There are about 2,000 tankers carrying oil across the world's oceans. This is about 1,000 fewer than in the peak year of 1977. However, today's tankers are larger than in the past. The danger of serious pollution if any one of the world's fleet of tankers has an accident is therefore greater.

▼ Fish and seabirds were killed in their thousands. Coastal resorts also suffered, losing money as their beaches were blackened with oil.

The *Ixtoc* oil blowout

1979

On June 3, 1979, there was a blowout on the *Ixtoc* oil rig in the sea off the Yucatán Peninsula in the Gulf of Mexico. Attempts to shut off the oil flow failed and the situation went out of control. By early August, a slick of thick crude oil 400 miles long was moving northward toward the southeastern coast of Texas. The final estimate was that over 210 million gallons had been released in the world's worst-ever oil spill.

Efforts to contain the oil slick and prevent it from reaching the coast were hampered by two factors. First, the wind kept changing. Second, the crude oil was so heavy that it sunk beneath the surface of the sea. This made tracing its progress difficult and allowed it to seep under the barriers (or booms) that had been laid on the surface in an attempt to contain the oil. By August 7, the slick was about 500 miles long. In the end, there was less damage than had at first been feared, although the effect on fish and seabirds was horrifying.

▲ An oil company employee checks part of the *Lindad del Carmen* oil rig, off the Mexican coast, in the same area as the *Ixtoc* rig.

Environmental experts say that about 924 million gallons of oil are released into the world's oceans each year. The biggest offenders in most years are oil tankers that either wash out their tanks at sea or leak oil after being wrecked.

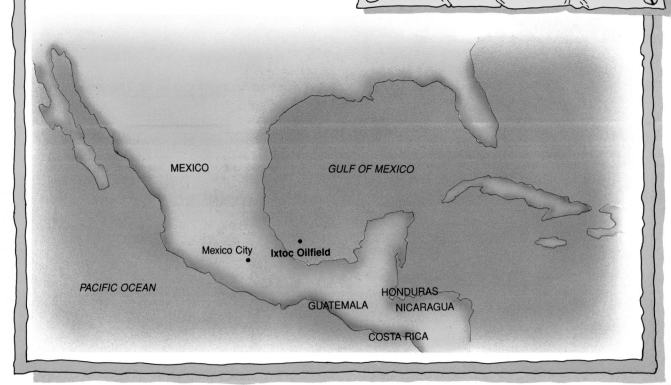

MEXICO

GULF OF MEXICO

Mexico City   **Ixtoc Oilfield**

PACIFIC OCEAN

HONDURAS

GUATEMALA   NICARAGUA

COSTA RICA

The Nowruz oilfield blowout

1983

"Catastrophic" was the word the World Wildlife Fund (now the World Wide Fund for Nature) used in July 1983 to describe events in the Persian Gulf.

In 1983, the Nowruz oilfield, off the Iranian coast, suffered one disaster after another. In February, crude oil began to gush from an oil rig that had been struck by a ship. Iraq, which was at war with Iran, blew up another rig on March 2. In all, as many as eight oil rigs may have been damaged in the fighting.

The bitter war between Iran and Iraq prevented attempts to repair the wells. The rest of the world looked on helplessly as 7,000 barrels (294,000 gallons) of oil a day flooded into the sea, coating the shores of the Persian Gulf in thick, sticky black oil. The effect on wildlife was devastating. There was also a severe water shortage, as governments had to close down the water purification plants that converted seawater into drinking water. By August, the oil was still flowing and experts warned that capping the leaking rigs would take another two months. The World Wildlife Fund said that it would take thirty years before the condition of the waters in the Gulf would return to normal.

> Wildlife casualties from the Nowruz blowouts included turtles, dolphins and sea snakes. However, the creature that was most seriously hit was the dugong or sea cow, which lives on seaweed. The World Wildlife Fund reported that almost the entire population of dugongs in the Persian Gulf had been wiped out by July 1983.

▼ When oil escapes into the sea, it sticks to everything. It is a long, hard operation clearing the beaches, and many fish and seabirds perish.

Bhopal chemical leak
1984

On the night of December 9, 1984, the people of Bhopal in central India went to bed as usual. The next day their city would be in the world's headlines.

During the night and through the early hours of December 10, 40 tons of deadly fumes leaked unnoticed from a storage tank at the Union Carbide chemical plant in the city. The fumes contained methyl isocyanate, a chemical used for making pesticides. As the suffocating cloud spread, thousands were killed, and many others suffered serious illnesses as a result. Although Union Carbide admitted responsibility for the disaster and paid compensation to the government, ten years later many victims were still awaiting payment.

Many industrial processes have been recognized as a cause of ill health. The damage can be sudden, as in Bhopal, or it may occur over a period of years. People working with some types of asbestos, for example, can die painfully from the after-effects of exposure up to forty years afterward.

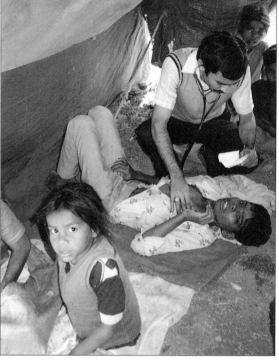

▲ The first to suffer were babies, children and people with breathing difficulties. Up to 250,000 people became seriously ill and many died later.

▼ People were still lining up for treatment over a year later. Kidney failure, blindness, and other serious effects were reported.

The Basle chemical spillage

1986

On November 1, 1986, there was a fire at a chemical plant beside the Rhine at Basle, Switzerland. While fighting the blaze, firemen flushed 30 tons of mercury and other poisonous chemicals into the Rhine. As a result, western Europe's largest waterway became a river of death. The Rhine turned red.

Within a week, half a million fish had died. Several tons of dead eels had been scooped from the riverbed. Waterworks that took water from the Rhine were sealed to prevent the poison from entering the human water supply. The river was affected along the whole of its course downstream from Basle in Switzerland through Germany to its mouth in the Netherlands. A massive cleanup operation began.

On January 19, 1987, it was reported that the Rhine was recovering and that in a further six months the river would be almost back to normal. Complete recovery would take until 1997.

The company that owned the chemical plant, Sandoz, admitted its responsibility for ignoring safety regulations in the storage of its dangerous chemicals. The Basle spillage led to a tightening-up of international rules on storage of such chemicals.

▼ The cleanup involved divers pumping up mud from the river bottom. The divers themselves had to be cleaned up when they came to the surface.

Chernobyl nuclear accident

1986

On the night of Friday, April 25, 1986, engineers at Chernobyl nuclear power station in the Ukraine, then part of the Soviet Union, slowed down the pumps that kept water in the station's cooling system flowing around the core of nuclear fuel. By about midnight, the temperature of the nuclear core had risen out of control. There was an explosion that blew up the building and sent red-hot radioactive dust high into the atmosphere.

Twenty-nine people in and around the power station were killed in the blast. A deadly radiation cloud spread westward across Europe. Despite the evacuation of cities in the Ukraine, hundreds of people became seriously ill with radiation sickness. All over Europe, food crops and animals that had been contaminated had to be destroyed. A huge area of the Ukraine is still too contaminated for people to live in and it will not be safe to farm for years.

▲ Dressed in protective clothing, workers check part of the concrete shield surrounding the reactor at Chernobyl.

In March 1979, the United States nearly experienced a disaster similar to the accident at Chernobyl. When the cooling system failed at the Three Mile Island nuclear power station in Pennsylvania, there was a leak of radioactive water and gas. Thousands of people were evacuated until the crisis had passed.

Piper Alpha
1988

Occidental Petroleum's oil rig *Piper Alpha* stood in the North Sea, 120 miles east of Wick, Scotland. On July 6, 1988, 227 workers were on board.

At about midnight, the rig was rocked by an explosion. The crew's well-drilled emergency procedures went into action, but ten minutes later there was another explosion. Escaping gas sent a ball of fire shooting across the production platform, and flames shot 500 feet into the air. Many crew members jumped 200 feet from the decks into the sea—but by this time the water itself was aflame.

The crews of the rescue helicopters and boats performed miracles of bravery and navigation, getting in close to the burning rig to pick up survivors. But the next day, it had to be reported that 157 of the *Piper Alpha*'s crew had died.

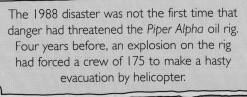

The 1988 disaster was not the first time that danger had threatened the *Piper Alpha* oil rig. Four years before, an explosion on the rig had forced a crew of 175 to make a hasty evacuation by helicopter.

▲ By the morning of July 7, 1988, all that remained of *Piper Alpha* was a tangled mass of wreckage.

◀ One of six helicopters hovers near the burning oil platform. Eventually seven warships and twenty-one other boats would join in the rescue attempt.

Hillsborough soccer disaster 1989

On April 15, 1989, thousands of fans arrived at Hillsborough soccer stadium in Sheffield, England. Liverpool was playing Nottingham Forest in the semifinal of the FA Cup.

When the referee blew the whistle for the kickoff, crowds of Liverpool supporters were still trying to get into the stadium. The police gave orders for a gate to be unlocked and the supporters poured through, racing through a tunnel to reach the stands in time to see the action. But the stands were already crowded.

As the extra spectators pushed in, people at the front of the stand were crushed against the fence, which had been put up to stop people running onto the field. Six minutes into the game, it was halted by the referee, but there was a fatal delay of several minutes before the fence gates around the field were opened to release the pressure. By that time, many fans had been crushed to death and more than 200 injured. The final death toll (including one victim who lingered for five years in a coma) was ninety-six. It was the worst disaster in British sports history.

Four years before the Hillsborough disaster, Liverpool fans were involved in a tragedy at the Heysel stadium in the Netherlands. Liverpool was playing an Italian club, Juventus, in the European Cup Final. Liverpool fans charged the Juventus supporters and trapped them against a wall, which collapsed. Thirty-five people died.

▲ Flowers and supporters' scarves were left at the gates of Liverpool's home field as tokens of remembrance of those who died.

◀ Some trapped spectators were able to get to safety by climbing up onto the grandstand balcony above.

The *Exxon Valdez* oil spill
1989

At 9 p.m. on March 24, 1989, the *Exxon Valdez*, a huge supertanker, sailed from Alaska with a full cargo of crude oil.

The *Exxon Valdez* was only three years old and was equipped with every modern navigational aid. Her captain knew the Alaskan waters well. Yet three hours after setting sail, the tanker was stuck fast on rocks, and 13.2 million gallons of oil were spilling out.

The oil spill covered 500 sq. miles of sea and was washed up along over 800 miles of coastline. Attempts to clean up the oil were hampered by delays in getting started, the remoteness of the site and the fact that the ground was frozen solid. Up to 30,000 seabirds, together with seals, other mammals and countless fish, died horribly within days of the disaster. Pollution also destroyed the feeding grounds of the thousands of migrating birds that cross Alaska twice a year.

▲ Workers gather boulders in buckets, before using high-pressure water jets to remove the oil. The cleanup was a lengthy and difficult operation.

Why did the *Exxon Valdez* disaster happen? An inquiry found that the captain had received permission from the Valdez harbor authorities to change course because of a threat of icebergs in the area. There was confusion over the new course to be set, and as a result the ship foundered on the rocks.

▼ High-pressure hoses were used to clean oil from rocks on the Alaskan coast.

The Aral Sea
today

The Aral Sea, once the world's fourth largest lake, lies across the border of Khazakstan and Uzbekistan in central Asia, about 400 miles from the city of Tashkent. It is the scene of one of the world's worst environmental disasters.

The problems result from the decision to use the area around the lake for cotton-growing. Large-scale schemes diverted river water to the fields to irrigate the crops. The result is that water from the rivers that used to drain into the Aral Sea no longer reaches it. Its water level has dropped more than 46 feet since 1960. In addition, huge amounts of pesticides and other agricultural chemicals were used to increase crop production, and these chemicals have drained into the seabed.

▲ Large parts of what was once the Aral Sea are now vast areas of mud. For much of the year the mud is dried and cracked, as it is here. What is more, the draining of pesticides into the soil makes this land virtually useless.

The Aral Sea has seen many changes in its level. For most of the nineteenth century the water level in the lake fell, but from 1880 onward it began to rise. By 1908, the level had risen by nearly 10 feet. Modern cotton-farming has now reversed this trend.

When the level of the lake dropped, these chemicals were exposed on the shore and have damaged the health of the people of the area. One terrible fact is that, around the Aral Sea, one in ten of all babies dies within its first year.

Experts say that if the shrinking of the Aral Sea continues at the present rate, there will be very little of it left by the year 2000.

◄ The dramatic drop in the water level of the Aral Sea is shown by these ships, once able to sail through waters that have disappeared, leaving the vessels uselessly grounded by the shore.

Soil erosion
today

Modern farming methods have greatly increased the productivity of the land. However, these methods can also cause lasting damage if they are not used wisely and within strict guidelines.

Basilicata is a mountainous region of southern Italy bordering the Gulf of Taranto in the Mediterranean. It is an area of steep clay slopes and deep valleys. Basilicata was once forested, but the trees have all been cleared. The invention of the tractor made it possible to plow many of the slopes for farming.

Because the rainfall in the area varies considerably from year to year, the soil dries out in years of low rainfall. Without the trees that used to hold the soil in place, the soil is quickly washed away when the rains come. Frequent mudslides damage roads, bridges and irrigation ditches. Slowly but surely, the farming land is being eroded away.

▲ In a place with variable rainfall, a slope like this can quickly turn from a dry area to a mudslide.

Damage to farmland can also cause problems in the city. Families who can no longer make a living from the land often move to the cities to try to find work. Even if they are able to find jobs, they are often forced to live in unhealthy, overcrowded and sometimes makeshift homes.

Deforestation in the Amazon
today

For hundreds of years people have been clearing land for farming near the Amazon in South America, but until this century this had little impact as the forests are so vast and the areas cleared were quite small. But modern machinery clears the forest far more quickly and ruthlessly than was possible with only hand-tools. Meanwhile, population growth in South America has produced a great increase in the demand for land for raising crops and cattle. Farmers move into the cleared forest land, but after a few years the the soil is exhausted and the farmers move on.

Trees use carbon dioxide and give off oxygen. Their destruction means that the carbon dioxide in the atmosphere is increasing. This is one cause of "global warming," which may eventually affect the world's climate and all our lives.

▲ Trees have been cleared here to make way for a settlement. New paved roads built nearby have encouraged people to move to this area.

Each minute of every day in the year, bulldozers clear an area of the world's tropical forests equal to the size of 200 soccer fields. At the present rate of destruction, the Amazon rainforest will have disappeared completely within 400 years.

▼ In southeastern Brazil, large areas of rainforest have been cleared to make space for a new railroad. This will also encourage people to settle nearby.

Acid rain
today

The smoke and gases released when "fossil" fuels, such as coal and oil, are burned and the waste gases produced by factories combine in the atmosphere to produce sulfuric and nitric acid. These chemicals collect in the clouds. The rain from these clouds often falls hundreds of miles from the source of pollution, and contains high levels of these acids.

Trees take in acid rain through their roots and leaves. It deforms their roots and stops the development of their branches and buds. Pine and other evergreen trees lose their needles. In the end, many trees die. The industrial areas of Britain, France and Belgium released millions of tons of sulfur into the air in the 1980s. Germany and Scandinavia lie in the path of the prevailing south-westerly winds that cross these areas. Their forests, rivers and lakes have suffered terrible damage from acid rain.

▲ These diseased and dying trees show the effects of acid rain in Germany. Together with the Scandinavian countries, Germany is the nation that has been most badly damaged by acid rain.

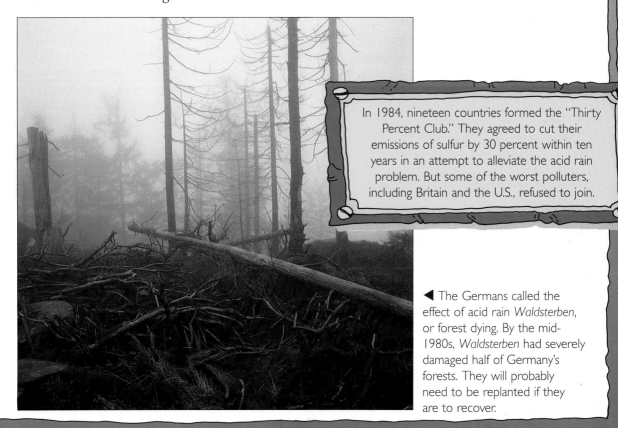

In 1984, nineteen countries formed the "Thirty Percent Club." They agreed to cut their emissions of sulfur by 30 percent within ten years in an attempt to alleviate the acid rain problem. But some of the worst polluters, including Britain and the U.S., refused to join.

◀ The Germans called the effect of acid rain *Waldsterben*, or forest dying. By the mid-1980s, *Waldsterben* had severely damaged half of Germany's forests. They will probably need to be replanted if they are to recover.

African rainforest clearance today

A great band of tropical rainforest stretches across west and central Africa. It provides a habitat for thousands of species of plant and animal life, including human forest-dwellers.

Rainforests also play an important part in maintaining the health of our planet. Evaporation of moisture from the forests into the atmosphere spreads water vapor and warmth away from the tropics to the cooler regions of the world. Plants take in carbon dioxide from the air, helping to keep world temperatures in check.

In West Africa, 13,500 sq. miles of forest are destroyed each year. In Ghana, the area of forest has declined from 40,000 sq. miles in 1960 to only 5,800 sq. miles today. The forest hardwoods are exported. The land is then cleared and used for farming. Many plant and animal species are threatened with extinction.

▲ In this section of West African rainforest, the only remains of the original vegetation are a few splinters of wood and a solitary tree defaced by graffiti.

The World Wide Fund for Nature (WWF) is one of the international organizations that are trying to preserve the rainforests. At Korup Park in Cameroon, West Africa, the WWF is trying to show how rainforests can be preserved while at the same time providing a living for their inhabitants.

It is easy to understand the clearances. The sale of hardwoods earns much-needed money for these countries. The growing population of West Africa needs land to farm to grow their food crops. But these are short-term gains at the expense of the whole world. The shrinking of Africa's forests could be a factor in a future world climatic disaster.

◀ Logs float down a river to be sold in Gabon, West Africa. Gabon's good-quality tropical hardwoods fetch high prices.

Salinization
today

Salinization is the slow poisoning of irrigated land by the deposit of salt. In many parts of the world, land can be made fit for farming only by irrigation—channeling water across it from rivers and streams. If drainage is poor and the land becomes waterlogged, the water dissolves salts from the soil, which can damage plant roots. In wet climates, rain washes the salts out before they can cause any damage, but in hot, dry regions this does not happen.

The buildup of salt can be severe enough to kill the crop plants. In some places so much salt has been deposited over the years that it can be seen as a white layer. The land often has to be abandoned for farming and returns to desert. Unfortunately, the problem is most serious in areas where farming land is scarce and large populations create a huge demand for food. In Iraq, as much as half of all the irrigated land is affected by salinization. In Egypt and Pakistan, one-third or more of irrigated land is affected, and salinization is an increasing problem in parts of the United States, China, Peru, Spain and Australia.

▲ In this former farmland in Egypt, salinization has occurred because the land was not properly drained. Now virtually nothing will grow here.

Almost one-third of the world's food is grown on irrigated land. Some scientists estimate that more irrigated land is being abandoned because of salinization than is being brought into use by new irrigation schemes.

◀ Surface water has built up in this Egyptian field because water from irrigation has not drained away. Eventually the water will evaporate in the heat, leaving the harmful salts behind.

The Ozone layer today

The ozone layer is a thin layer of gas in the stratosphere between 10 and 30 miles above the Earth's surface. It makes life possible by filtering out dangerous radiation—especially ultraviolet rays—from the Sun.

Instruments on satellites allow the thickness and extent of the ozone layer to be measured. These observations show an increasing "hole" in the layer over Antarctica. If increased amounts of harmful radiation reach the Earth, the effects on plant and animal life could be disastrous. One result could be an increase in cases of skin cancer.

The changes in the ozone layer are partly caused by CFCs, chemicals that are often used in aerosols, refrigerators, dry cleaning and the manufacture of certain plastics. Today, many manufacturers use different "ozone-friendly" chemicals in their products.

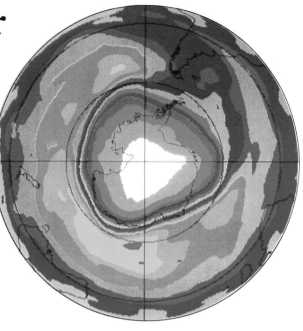

▲ This map shows the ozone "hole." In 1986, there was only half as much ozone there as there had been thirty years before.

It is not only over the Antarctic that the ozone layer has been affected. In 1988, it was found that ozone over the northern hemisphere was 3 percent thinner than twenty years before. This change is enough to cause an increase in cases of skin cancer.

▼ Because of the "hole" in the ozone layer, people are advised to wear hats and plenty of sunscreen.

The Tay Bridge collapse
1879

The Tay Bridge carries the main railroad line between London and Aberdeen over the Firth of Tay on the east coast of Scotland. The first Tay Bridge was two miles long. At the time of its opening in May 1878, it was the longest bridge in the world.

At about 7 p.m. on the evening of December 28, 1879, two signalmen at the southern end of the bridge watched as the Dundee-bound mail train steamed past them. The wind was blowing fiercely. As they watched, they saw a shower of sparks fly up from the middle of the bridge, followed by a brilliant flash of light and then total darkness.

Despite the bad weather, they rushed down to the shore to try to find out what had happened. A brief shaft of moonlight between the clouds showed that the middle section of the bridge was missing. The train, with its seventy-nine passengers, had vanished beneath the waters of the Firth.

An inquiry found that the bridge had been badly engineered and placed the blame on its designer, Sir Thomas Bouch. He became the eightieth victim of the disaster, dying soon after the inquiry's report was published.

Sir Thomas Bouch had already designed a railroad bridge for eastern Scotland's other great Firth, the Firth of Forth. Fortunately, it was never built. Later calculations showed that he had allowed for a wind strength only one-twelfth of what was needed. The Forth railroad bridge, built to a new design, was opened in 1890.

▼ After the Tay Bridge collapsed, divers went down to try to find the train. They were unable to rescue any of the passengers.

The sinking of the *Titanic*

1912

People said that she was unsinkable. The largest passenger ship afloat, the *Titanic* was built with watertight compartments below deck. The ship would stay afloat even if up to three of these were flooded.

On April 11, 1912, the *Titanic* set out from Southampton on her maiden voyage to New York. On board were 2,224 people, including a crew of 800. The ship forged westward, making good progress for three days and nights.

At about midnight on the fourth night, off the coast of Newfoundland, the *Titanic* collided at full speed with a huge iceberg. Below decks, six of the *Titanic's* watertight compartments had been breached, and water was pouring in. The unthinkable had happened—the unsinkable ship was sinking.

▲ When the *Titanic* struck the iceberg off Newfoundland, evacuation of the ship began, but there was a shortage of lifeboats and panic grew among the passengers. In the end, 1,513 people went down with the ship as her stern rose and she slid to the bottom of the Atlantic Ocean.

In 1985, over seventy years after the sinking of the *Titanic*, underwater exploration teams located the wreckage and began to explore it. Plans to raise the ship have never been carried out. Many people believe that the *Titanic* should be left where it is as a memorial to whose who died.

Bagmati Railroad Crash
1981

On June 6, 1981, a train traveling from Samastipur to Banmukhi in Bihar, India plunged off a bridge into the Bagmati River.

Bihar is a densely populated state in northeastern India, and the country's poorest. Most of its inhabitants have very little education and cannot read or write. In this situation it is not surprising that people cannot afford to pay fares to travel, that there is too little public transport, that trains and tracks are not looked after properly, and that there is no money to pay people to check that safety rules are followed.

It is common in the poorer parts of India for trains to be massively overcrowded, with passengers clinging to the outer sides of the train or sitting on its roof. So it was at Bagmati.

The official number of dead was put at 268, but many authorities claimed that the actual figure was more than 800, and could have been over a thousand. This made it the worst rail disaster of all time.

The second worst rail disaster happened on June 4, 1989, at Chelyabinsk in the then Soviet Union. Two passenger trains on the Trans-Siberian railway, one of them crowded with vacationers bound for Black Sea resorts, were destroyed by exploding liquid gas from a nearby pipeline. Between 600 and 800 people died.

◀ An aerial view showing the wreckage of the train, most of which fell into the River Bagmati.

The *R101* airship

1930

In the 1920s, winged aircraft had a short range and could carry few passengers. But airships carried people in a compartment suspended under a gas-filled "balloon" (see the top picture opposite), and were considered by some to be the passenger aircraft of the future. In 1919, after a British airship made a double crossing of the Atlantic, a non-stop airship flight from Britain to India was planned. A big new airship, the *R101*, was built.

On October 4, 1930, the *R101* set out from London with fifty-three passengers on board. Heading southeast across the English Channel, the airship ran into heavy winds. Suddenly, near Beauvais, northwest of Paris, the *R101*

▲ Amongst the wreckage of the *R101*, one of its huge engines is clearly visible.

encountered a heavier squall. The nose of the airship tilted, and it plunged toward the ground. As it smashed through the trees of a forest, it burst into flames, which shot 295 feet into the air. Only five people escaped.

The disaster so shocked the British people that the government decided to end its airship program.

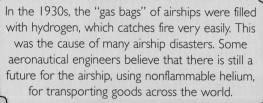

In the 1930s, the "gas bags" of airships were filled with hydrogen, which catches fire very easily. This was the cause of many airship disasters. Some aeronautical engineers believe that there is still a future for the airship, using nonflammable helium, for transporting goods across the world.

The *Hindenburg*

1937

After the *R101* disaster (see opposite) and a crash involving the American airship *Akron* in 1933, only Germany continued to build airships for passenger use. In 1936, the German airship the *Hindenburg* made the first of several transatlantic flights. Over 787 feet long, it was the largest airship ever built. Its passengers traveled in great comfort and luxury at 180 mph.

The *Hindenburg's* designer, Hugo Eckener, had wanted its "balloon" to be filled with helium gas, which was safer than the usual hydrogen. However, helium was only manufactured in the United States, and the Americans feared that if it were supplied to Germany, it might be used for making weapons. It was a fateful decision.

On May 6, 1937, the *Hindenburg* approached its mooring tower at Lakehurst, New Jersey, after a flight from Germany. Suddenly, at about 7:30 p.m., it burst into flames, trapping many passengers and killing thirty-six of them.

▲ The *Hindenburg* made ten successful trips across the Atlantic Ocean, carrying passengers from Frankfurt to Lakehurst, New Jersey. Here it flies over the skyscrapers of New York City on its way to Lakehurst.

The *Hindenburg* disaster ended Germany's airship program, and it also ended the use of hydrogen for the few airships—mostly for military purposes —that were built afterward. It closed a chapter in luxury flying.

The *Hindenburg* tragedy made a huge impression on the American public because the airship's arrival was being described live on air by a radio journalist. His horror as it caught fire was carried direct into millions of American homes, one of the first eyewitness radio reports of a disaster.

▶ The airship rapidly turned into an orange fireball when it was only yards away from its mooring tower at Lakehurst.

The sinking of *Le Surcouf*
1942

When the French submarine *Le Surcouf* was completed in 1932, it was the largest submarine and one of the most advanced fighting machines in the world. It was armed with ten torpedo tubes, two 8-inch guns in a single turret and two antiaircraft guns, and it also carried twenty-two torpedoes. A small hangar on board housed a seaplane, which could be used to search for the victims of merchant ship accidents.

It was, tragically, a merchant ship that brought disaster to *Le Surcouf*. Then in the service of the Free French during World War II, *Le Surcouf* was sailing through Caribbean waters when it was accidentally rammed and sunk by the American merchant ship SS *Thompson Lykes* on February 18, 1942. There was not a single survivor among the 130 officers and men who had been on board the submarine. It was the world's worst submarine disaster.

▲ *Le Surcouf* tied up at Cherbourg, France, during an inspection by the French President in July 1933. The armored turret is clearly visible toward the stern.

A submarine has an inner and an outer hull. To make the vessel sink, the space between these is filled with water; to make it rise, water is emptied out. A hole in the inner hull of a submarine will wreck it, as it would any other ship.

The worst British disaster involving a submarine occurred on June 1, 1939, when HMS *Thetis* was sunk during trials in Liverpool, with the loss of 99 lives.

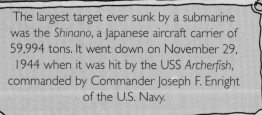

The largest target ever sunk by a submarine was the *Shinano*, a Japanese aircraft carrier of 59,994 tons. It went down on November 29, 1944 when it was hit by the USS *Archerfish*, commanded by Commander Joseph F. Enright of the U.S. Navy.

▼ *Le Surcouf* sails proudly out of harbor, going out on patrol during the 1930s.

Paris air crash
1974

The Turkish Airlines DC-10 flight left Paris for London on March 3, 1974. After just a few minutes, the burning wreckage of the aircraft lay in the Forest of Ermonville, north of Paris. All 346 passengers and crew were dead.

Eyewitnesses saw the aircraft flying fast and low toward the forest before it was torn apart in a massive fireball. The burning wreckage tore a track almost 1 mile long through the trees. Searchers discovered later that not all the wreckage was in the forest. They found more debris and bodies 7 miles away.

Investigations showed that the door to the cargo hold had blown off in midair, causing the DC-10 to crash and causing some people to be sucked out.

▲ Priests of various denominations at the funeral service for the 351 victims of the Turkish Airlines DC-10 disaster. At the time it was called "the worst air crash the world has yet known."

The wide-bodied McDonnell Douglas DC-10 has three turbofan engines, one beneath each wing and the third mounted on the tail. In 1974, there were about 130 DC-10s in service with the world's airlines.

Tenerife airport crash

1977

On March 27, 1977, an American Pan Am Boeing 747 had been cleared for take-off from Tenerife in the Canaries. It turned on to the main airport runway. Too late, the pilot realized that there was another Boeing 747, a Dutch KLM aircraft, on the runway ahead of him.

Unable to stop in time, the taxiing Pan Am jet smashed into the KLM Boeing, killing all 248 people on the Dutch aircraft. The fully loaded fuel tanks in the wings of both aircraft exploded in flames. On the Pan Am plane, seventy people survived, but most had horrific burns. The total death toll was 574.

The disaster was the tragic result of confusion, which had begun with a bomb explosion at the airport at Las Palmas, the Canaries' other main island. Because of this emergency, both jumbos had been diverted to Tenerife. In the chaos that followed, the pilot of the KLM jet had tried to take off without clearance from air traffic control.

▲ Personal possessions of the crash victims were piled up on the runway at Tenerife. The collision was the worst disaster in aviation history.

▼ Spanish servicemen help to clear up the wreckage of the two aircraft. There was no hope of finding any survivors by this time.

The huge Boeing 747 made its first appearance in 1970, and by 1973 there were 220 in regular service. The 747 can carry up to 500 passengers, cruising at 580 mph.

Challenger space shuttle

1986

At noon on January 28, 1986, millions of Americans settled down to watch the launch of the space shuttle *Challenger* on television. It was the twenty-fifth space shuttle flight, but this one was special. The seven people on board—five men and two women—included Christa McAuliffe, a schoolteacher who had volunteered for the U.S. government's "citizens in space" program. Her husband and children, with the families of the other crew members, were among the television audience.

Just seventy-three seconds after lift-off, the viewers' smiles turned to cries of horror as they saw *Challenger* explode. There was no hope of saving the crew. The disaster was caused by a faulty seal on a booster rocket. The leak had ignited shortly after lift-off and the flames spread rapidly to the main fuel tank.

▲ Traveling at nearly 2,000 mph, *Challenger* exploded into a fireball. The remains of the shuttle fell into the Atlantic Ocean, where they were later recovered by U.S. Navy divers.

▼ *Challenger* exploded in midair, 72 miles above the launch-pad at Cape Canaveral.

The seven crew of the *Challenger* were the American space program's first casualties in space. In 1967, three American astronauts were killed on the launch pad when their spacecraft caught fire before lift-off.

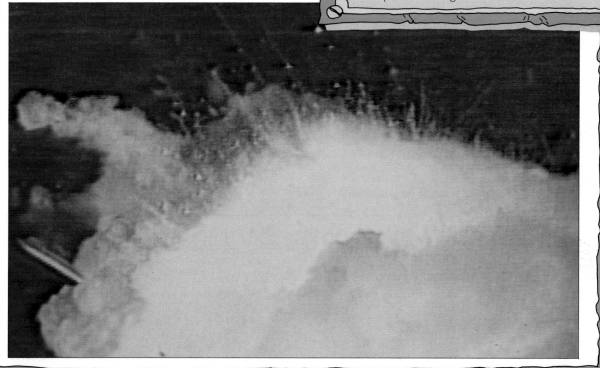

The Philippines ferry collision
1987

On December 21, 1987, the ferry *Doña Paz* was carrying a full load of passengers to Manila from Tacloban, in the Philippines, for Christmas. It was a dark, moonless night, but the weather was fine. The *Doña Paz* was only a few hours' sailing from its destination when, in the dark of the early hours, it collided with the oil tanker *Victor*. The two ships exploded in a ball of fire, and flaming oil burst over the sea. Both ships sank almost at once.

No one will ever know how many ferry passengers died that night. The passenger list of the *Doña Paz* contained about 1,550 names, but there were many more on board—possibly as many as 4,000. The *Doña Paz* collision was certainly the world's worst-ever shipping disaster.

▲ Local people removed bodies from the water after the sinking of the *Doña Paz*. The number of bodies suggested that the ship probably contained twice as many people as she was licensed to carry.

The waters around the Philippine islands are among the most dangerous in the world because they are overcrowded with shipping and due to fierce storms that often occur there. Between 1972 and 1987, there were eighty reported collisions in the area and 117 sinkings.

▼ A Philippines navy vessel scoured the area of the disaster, looking for survivors. It found none, but another boat picked up twenty-six people.

The Baltic ferry sinking

1994

At 7 p.m. on September 28, 1994, the "roll-on roll-off" ferry *Estonia* left Talinn in Estonia for the twelve-hour crossing of the Baltic Sea to Stockholm in Sweden. Ninety minutes into the voyage, the ship hit heavy seas, but continued at full speed. Many passengers went to sleep.

Four hours later, one of the ship's engineers noticed water coming in through the bow doors. The pumps were switched on—but were not powerful enough to cope with the amount of water now pouring in. At about 2:00 a.m., the *Estonia*, hopelessly crippled with the weight of water inside her, capsized. At least 910 people—most of them Swedish—were drowned.

▲ Passengers took to small life rafts as the ship capsized. The disaster occurred when the doors at the front of the ship broke away during the storm.

As a result of the Baltic ferry disaster engineers have been reevaluating the design of roll-on roll-off ferries, so that these ships can be made more stable in the event that water enters the lower decks.

▼ Rescue teams in military helicopters picked up as many survivors as they could find.

Word Strings

R	I	A	F	I	N
T	O	T	M	E	E
E	E	E	O	D	R
M	F	L	O	F	I

There are four words in this rectangle connected with disasters. Start at the bottom left corner and move from here to any other touching square (up, down, sideways or diagonally) until you have spelled out the words here:

M _ _ _ _ _ _ _ _ _ _ _

F _ _ _ _ _

F _ _ _ _

F _ _ _

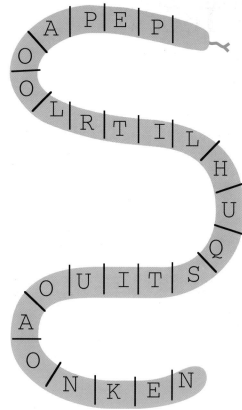

There are three words in the snake connected with disasters. The words are jumbled together, but the letters in each word are in the right order. Start at the snake's head and see if you can find:

EA _ _ _ _ _ _ _ _

PO _ _ _ _ _ _ _

PO _ _ _ _

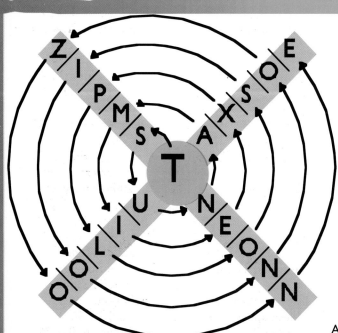

Start in the middle of the windmill and work outward to find three more words connected with disasters. They are:

O _ _ _ E

T _ _ _ _ _ I

E _ _ _ _ _ _ N

Answers can be found on page 111 at the back of the book

Index

Picture Acknowledgments

a = above l = left
b = below r = right
Ardea: 10a & b (François Gohier), 9b (Mina Carpi), 56a (D. Parer & E. Parer Cook), 56b (Jean-Paul Ferrero), 59a (John Clegg), **Associated Press:** 23a, 25a & b, 34a, 42a & b, 87a. **Biofotos:** 50a & b (Andrew Henley), 69a (G. Kinns), 69b (Andrew Henley), 75a. **Bridgeman Art Library:** 11a & b (Victoria and Albert Museum), 15b (O'Shea Gallery, London), 27b (Musée des Beaux-Arts, Le Havre), 49a (Private Collection), 49b (Private Collection), 53b (Guildhall Library, Corporation of London), 58 (Church of San Vitale, Ravenna). **Camera Press:** 3a & b, 24a & b (N. Blickov), 34b (Aeberli), 47a (August Sycholt), 51b, 74a (Ray Hamilton) 74b (Martin Peternotte), 76a (Shisei Kuwabara), 80a & b (Adrian Heitmann), 81a & b & 83

(Eulogio Munoz), 88a & b, 91a & b, 98b, 101a, 104a & b, 107a & b (Jonas Lemberg/Pressens Bild). **Corbis-Bettman:** 16a, 18a & b, 20b, 41a & b, 47b, 72a & b; (Reuter) 52a & b; (UPI) 2r, 21a & b, 22a & b, 32a & b, 43a, 51a, 54a & b, 66a & b., 67b, 70, 77a & b, 78, 84a & b, 99a & b, 101, 105a & b. **E.T. Archive:** 35a, 35b. **Mary Evans Picture Library:** 98a **Robert Harding:** 73a (Ian Griffiths), 73b, 93b. **Hulton Deutsch:** 3a, 14b, 16b, 20a, 23b, 26, 31a, 38b (Reuters), 39a & b, 44a & b, 53a, 62b, 63a & b, 68b, 103a & b. **Hutchison:** 36a & b (Sarah Errington), 46a & b (S. Errington), 48a, 48b (Hilly James), 55b, 57a (John Ryle), 57b (Dr Nigel Smith), 61 (Adrian Evans), 64a (Nancy Durrell McKenna), 68a (Leslie Woodhead), 82, 86a, 90a, b (V. Ivleva), 92b

(Richard House), 93a & b (Michael MacIntyre), 94b (Bernard Régent), 95a & b (Sarah Errington). **Illustrated London News Picture Library:** 97b, 100a & b, 102a & b. **Popperfoto:** 37a & b, 65a & b, 85a & b, 105a & b. **Royal Geographical Society:** 17, 19 71. **Science Photo Library:** 2b (NASA), 8 (David A. Hardy), 9a (Julian Baum), 12 (Pekka Parriainen), 13a & b (Novosti), 27a (Roger Ressmeyer /Starlight), 28a (Gianni Tortoli), 28b (Geospace), 28b (Gregory Dimjian), 30a (Matthew Shipp), 30b (NASA), 33a (Professor Stewart Lowther), 33b (Vincent Realmuto), 38a (Earth Satellite Corporation), 40a (Brian Brake), 40b (Novosti), 45a (NRSC Ltd), 45b James Stevenson), 59b (Jean-Loup Charmet), 60a (National Library of Medicine), 60b (Jean-Loup Charmet), 62a (National Library of Medicine), 64b (Alfred Pasieka), 67a

NIBSC), 86b (Novosti), 89a & b (Vanessa Vick), 92a (Dr Morley Read), 94a (Françoise Sauze), 96a (NASA).

Front cover (clockwise from top left): Ardea (François Gohier); Camera Press (N. Blickov); Camera Press (August Sycholt); Corbis-Bettmann/UPI; Science Photo Library (Roger Ressmeyer/ Starlight); Science Photo Library (NRSC Ltd); Range/Bettmann; Camera Press; Ardea (Mina Carpi); Science Photo Library (Gianni Tortoli); Corbis-Bettmann/UPI; Science Photo Library (NIBSC). *Back cover (clockwise from top left):* Hulton Deutsch; Bridgeman Art Library (Musée des Beaux-arts, Le Havre); Camera Press; Bridgeman Art Library (Private Collection); Ardea (John Clegg); Corbis-Bettmann; Hutchison Library; Hutchison Library; Science Photo Library (NASA).